Finding Your
SOUL MATE

Other titles by Paul Fenton-Smith

Astrology Revealed
Palmistry Revealed
The Tarot Revealed
A Secret Door to the Universe
Mastering the Tarot

Finding Your SOUL MATE

PAUL FENTON-SMITH

SIMON & SCHUSTER
AUSTRALIA

Dedicated to Alexander for the joy you bring to our lessons.

With thanks to Cathy for her help in editing the early drafts
and to all those who generously replied to my questionnaire
and shared their life experiences.

FINDING YOUR SOUL MATE

First published in Australia in 2001 by
Simon & Schuster Australia
20 Barcoo Street, East Roseville NSW 2069

A Viacom Company
Sydney New York London Toronto Tokyo Singapore

National Library of Australia
Cataloguing-in-Publication data

 Fenton-Smith, Paul.
 Finding your soul mate.

 ISBN 0 7318 1013 9.

 1. Soul mates. 2. Interpersonal relations – Psychic
 aspects. 3. Interpersonal relations – Miscellanea. I.
 Title.

 133.9

Cover design: Anna Soo
Internal design: Avril Makula
Set in 11.5pt Revival
Printed in Australia by Griffin Press

10 9 8 7 6 5 4 3 2 1

Contents

❧

Chapter One

WHAT IS A SOUL MATE?

Your soul's fate

WHILE MANY OF US SEARCH FOR OUR SOUL MATE, MAKING CAREFUL LISTS OF THE DESIRED QUALITIES THAT WE ARE LOOKING FOR IN THAT RIGHT PERSON, WE NEED TO REMEMBER THAT WE, TOO, ARE PROBABLY BEING SOUGHT OUT BY OTHERS. We are being described in the lists that others are making, and so we only have half the work to do in finding our soul mate, as they are seeking us out also. This book examines some of the steps we need to take to prepare ourselves for a soul-mate love relationship, including knowing what qualities we possess and what we can bring to a love relationship. What you have to offer others is what makes you desirable to them.

In the search for the deepest love relationship possible, this term 'soul mate' is often used, perhaps more often than it warrants. But what exactly is a soul mate?

When I asked a random selection of people this question, they described a soul mate as 'someone who is meant to be with you for life', 'your spiritual partner', 'your life partner' and 'your spiritual other half'. While all of these descriptions can be partly true, to fully understand the meaning of the term 'soul mate', one has to examine the possible purpose of the soul.

The soul or spirit is a term often used to describe that essence of a person which animates the human body. Although we may not be able to pinpoint the soul or spirit in a person, we are certainly aware of its absence when the person dies and we are left only with the physical body. If you accept the philosophy of reincarnation, which suggests that the soul experiences successive lives in different physical bodies, then it follows that it is possible to subconsciously 'recognise' a soul from a past life shared together, despite the different physical body it inhabits this lifetime.

Buddhists have long held the belief in reincarnation and have documented cases, including the identification of the current (14th) Dalai Lama in the book *Kundun* (Mary Craig, HarperCollins London, 1997). In this case a two-year-old boy living in the village of Takster, high on the Tibetan plateau, was believed to be the reincarnation of the Dalai Lama and to test if this was the case, several monks travelled from Lhasa to visit him. The journey took months and they travelled in disguise so as not to alert others to their true purpose. When they arrived, posing as traders, they asked for lodging for the night and were well received. Soon after arriving they presented the boy with items which belonged to the deceased 13th Dalai Lama, among items belonging to living monks. The boy recognised the monks immediately despite having never met nor heard about them before and correctly identified the items belonging to the deceased Lama. He also correctly named three of the visiting monks who were unknown to him or his parents, and he then asked the monks if they were ready to take him home (to Lhasa, and to his monastery). It was then that the boy's mother told them how long he had been waiting for the men to come from 'far away to take me home'.

In most cases when you meet a soul mate, such clarity of information is uncommon, but it is usual for you to feel an inner sense of recognition, as though you have met before but you cannot seem to recall where or when it was. You recognise the energy of the person but not their presentation (their physical body), because they had a different body last time you knew them.

As I see it, soul mates are people whose life paths are shared for a period of time in order to learn spiritual lessons. Soul mates can be friends, lovers, family members or business partners. Confirmation of a soul-mate friendship or love relationship may be found in the intensity of that relationship from the start, or in the inner knowledge that destiny had a hand in bringing you together.

Through clinical hypnosis I have regressed many clients into a state where they can access past-life information related to fears, phobias and issues in this lifetime. At first I was sceptical about the existence of past lives but eventually reached the conclusion that if such methods resolved the present life's fears and phobias, then so be it.

It was only through my own experiences of past-life regression that I began to seek more clarity in this area. I read books but found it wasn't enough, as I was only getting second-hand experiences. In hypnosis sessions with a colleague, I found an increasing awareness of being fated towards a purpose, which was taking many lifetimes. Some part of me seemed to be aware of the very distant past and of a future too far forward to contemplate without feeling insecure about my present reality.

After years of using hypnosis for regressing clients, I have come to conclude that the term 'soul mate' signifies someone of either gender, any age, nationality or cultural background, who has shared a previous life (or part thereof) with you. In short, someone who shares a part of your soul's journey toward spiritual enlightenment or understanding. This means that your soul mate could have been your mother or father, your brother or sister, your business partner or your spiritual teacher, in a previous lifetime. So, too, they may have been your enemy, your torturer, the partner who broke your heart or the child whose birth saw the end of your own life.

This book deals with how soul mates affect our lives and how to identify the spiritual lessons they offer us. Although you may recognise the lessons contained within a friendship or love relationship, you are not obliged to learn those lessons, as you are free to decline the offer and say 'perhaps next lifetime'.

So why do so many of us spend much of our lives searching for that special person; that one solitary soul who knows from whence we came and where we are heading in this life, and in the next two or three?

As a clairvoyant, I am constantly faced with the question 'When will I meet my soul mate?' Some clients are afraid that they will miss meeting and being with their soul mate, while others have a deeper concern. They are concerned that they will not be ready and equipped to deal with the lessons offered to them when their soul mate arrives. This concern sometimes arises out of not having been ready to make the most of several previous soul-mate opportunities. Although new opportunities arrived, the current ones didn't re-present themselves if they were avoided or squandered. In some cases of lost opportunities between soul mates, the relationship collapsed due to fear – fear of not being loved, or the fear of being loved and then abandoned. For some, the deepest fear is that of simply being loved and discovered by another person.

So when clients ask me when they'll meet their soul mate, I ask them what they are doing to make themselves ready for their soul mate. I ask them if they are ready to be someone who can spiritually advance their new partner, or are they simply seeking someone to make their unhappy lives worthwhile.

If your soul mate is someone who has shared a part of your soul's journey so far, then they can be a parent, a friend, a neighbor or a partner. Taking this a step further, if you have lived for example, 160 lives so far, it is likely that you'll have had partners for at least half of those lives. So you'll have up to 80 souls from which to choose to be your soul mates in this lifetime.

It is unlikely that many of these souls will have been born in the same decade as yourself, or that you'll even find them in this crowded world. But they can be found, and they'll sometimes find you when you least expect it.

While some of us look searchingly for our next soul mate, others realise that it is the inner searching which matters most, and when we need someone to walk with us up some of the steps on our path, they will arrive.

Too often, modern romantic notions of a soul mate prevail, leading many to believe that the effortless, perfect love relationship lies out there if they could find it. All relationships require some work from time to time and it is not uncommon for partners to abandon love relationships because they felt that a particular partner couldn't have been their soul mate because things weren't always running smoothly.

The term soul mate can be seen as referring to someone who shares your soul purpose, often having shared some of your distant past. There are many different forms of relationship you can have with a soul mate, and these different relationships are examined in depth as we explore what we can do to improve our soul-mate relationships, and relationships generally. To begin, it is appropriate to examine your attitude to love relationships. In Chapter 4, you'll have a chance to decide what love means to you, and to determine if you want to continue to believe what you have always believed about love. Using the metaphor of boat building to represent the process of building a lasting love relationship, it offers a short lesson in boat building to enable you to glimpse the relationships you repeatedly build for yourself.

Chapter Two

FINDING PROOF OF YOUR PAST LIVES SHARED

IT IS EASY TO STATE THAT YOU HAVE SPENT TIME TOGETHER IN PREVIOUS LIVES, BUT IT REQUIRES A GREAT DEAL OF EFFORT TO CONFIRM SUCH A CLAIM. Often, distraught partners who have recently concluded a relationship, claim that they have just lost their soul mate, in order to give weight to their suffering. We suffer when we lose a partner, regardless of whether we have shared past lives with that person, because we have shared time in this life with them. We have shared hopes, dreams, plans and expectations, so it stands to reason that deep disappointment follows such a loss.

Somehow, with our Western pursuit of romantic love, many people develop the idea that a love relationship with their soul mate will be smooth sailing. It is through examining our past lives that we glimpse all the unfinished business with our soul mates.

In some cases, clients I have regressed into past lives reawaken their memories of all the pain, betrayals and the eventual abandonment, and they leave the session reluctant to pursue the soul-mate relationship in case it repeats some of those past patterns. An example of this occurred with Hannah.

Hannah came for a past-life regression to explore if and when she had spent any time with her current partner, George. Using hypnosis, we explored several lifetimes and found three that Hannah had shared with George. She recognised George by his unmistakable energy and in two of those lives she was the female partner and in the third shared life she was the man. In none of them did things end up pleasantly.

In the first life shared together, George died away at war while she was pregnant with his child. Hannah told me that she was about 15 or 16 years old at the time. In the second life shared together, George was a fisherman. He sailed away early each morning, not arriving home until late. He pursued other women and spent his nights drinking and gambling while she waited for him at home. After he drowned during a storm one morning, Hannah was left to fend for herself, which was not easy for a woman without an income. In the third life shared together, Hannah was the male; an ambitious soldier, spending much of his time working out ways to achieve promotion. In doing so, this soldier was ignoring his partner and even appeared contemptuous of her needs. His partner died of fever while he was away and it was then that he realised the things he had missed in that relationship and in life.

Hannah's history with George was typical of many of the past-life regressions I have conducted. Today relationships have a better chance of survival and can offer greater fulfilment, probably because we have more opportunity for better communication skills and knowledge about relationships than at any other time in history. It stands to reason that we are in a better position to have a fulfilling relationship now than in any other previous lifetime. In addition, most of our material needs are taken care of in basic terms. We don't have the daily threat of wild animals stealing out of the jungle to wreak havoc on our small village. We have more leisure opportunities than in previous times, and more wealth to spend on our loved ones during this free time.

In three shared past lives, Hannah and George had not fulfilled their goals for a love relationship, and they were together again for another attempt at a long-term love relationship. Hannah left that session feeling nervous about their chances, but with a better understanding of why each partner currently felt that the other's career ambitions was getting in the way of their shared goals. It was their dim memory of past lives spent pursuing goals instead of love that echoed around their current love relationship.

Although Hannah and George knew from the moment they met that they wanted to be together in a love relationship, all those past patterns were re-surfacing to be sorted out. More history shared together can mean more outstanding issues.

While most people are searching for someone who shares their history, others are searching for someone new, so they can both start afresh, with their present maturity and understanding of life. There's a lot to be said for meeting someone who doesn't know how selfish or stubborn you have been in previous lives!

There are several tried and trusted methods for accessing past lives, in order to see for yourself where you have been and with whom you spent your time. The following list details the strengths and weaknesses of each method.

1. Clairvoyance

Consulting a clairvoyant is probably the quickest method for ascertaining if you've spent time in previous lives with your present life friend or partner. It is advisable to consult a clairvoyant who specialises in past lives, or you may end up being told that you were a prince or a princess, and that you were very attractive, wealthy and indeed all the things that massage the ego. It won't necessarily be accurate, but it will make for good dinner party conversation.

Everyone likes to think that they were someone famous in a past life but I always ask people this: 'Where are all the past-life Roman viaduct builders, the slaves, the bread makers and the prostitutes? Where are all the real people?'

The benefit of consulting a clairvoyant for confirmation of past lives shared together is that it is quick and relatively effortless. The drawbacks include not being able to gauge the accuracy of the information you are receiving, and not being able to access that information directly.

You may visit the same clairvoyant six or seven times, each time being told a different story. The clairvoyant may say that they are accessing different lives, or different parts of a particular life, during each visit. This is quite possible, but accuracy is ensured when you can return to a particular lifetime in several sessions and retrieve more information each time, having confirmed what you've already seen in earlier sessions.

2. Past-life regression through hypnosis

This has the advantage of putting you 'in the lifetime you are returning to', by helping to access hidden memories of previous lives. During a deep state of hypnosis you are often able to access memories ordinarily unavailable to you in the waking state.

In most cases you can see (in your mind's eye), hear, feel, taste and smell everything that is going on around and within you. This is a very powerful technique for accessing past lives, but the drawback to this is when you are regressed to a painful situation, you'll feel it in all its intensity as though it was happening to you at that very moment.

In hypnosis, you can re-experience your past lives directly, with the guidance of the hypnotherapist. It is inadvisable to attempt past-life regression using self-hypnosis, as you can get yourself into difficulties that require the assistance of an independent outsider to get you through. This occurred with a friend and myself in 1986 when we were studying hypnosis. Using one another for practice, we started experimenting with past-life regression. One afternoon I regressed Claudia back to a life in ancient Egypt and she started to panic. Her breathing changed and her heart started racing. Her temperature increased until she was covered in perspiration and I repeatedly tried to soothe her and to identify what was happening but she was immersed in the life there and overcome with emotion.

Remembering my hypnosis training, I took her deeper into hypnosis and back further in time to another life, from which she was easily able to return to the present. If Claudia had been using self-hypnosis to regress herself, she may have been traumatised by being stuck in that life and those circumstances for hours at a time.

After the session she explained what was happening. (Usually the hypnotherapist is asking 'What is happening now?' continuously throughout the session to record details for discussion later.) She was a boy of about 12 years, and she went directly back to the closing moments of that boy's life.

The tradition was that the servants of rulers were sometimes buried alive with the deceased king (or Pharaoh), in order to help him towards the next life. This young boy was encased up to his waist in a clay/concrete type of solution and left to die as the tomb was sealed shut. Naturally he was terrified at the thought of impending death, and Claudia was feeling all of those emotions as she lay there on the mattress in hypnosis.

So hypnotic regression is not for the faint of heart, as powerful emotions can sweep through you during a past-life regression. Hypnotherapists vary in their techniques and in how they approach past-life regression but the process is essentially the same. I prefer to take each client through their death at the end of each life they have been regressed to, in order that they might lose some of their fear of death and so that they may review that lifetime.

After the soul has departed the physical body, I ask the client if they can tell me what they came to learn in that life and if they completed their lessons. The lessons are often simple things, like learning to trust again or learning the value of consistent effort towards your goals or even patience. If the lesson was not mastered in that lifetime, it is possible that they still have that lesson to learn in this life.

The drawback with hypnosis is that it takes time and requires effort. I usually take three one-hour sessions to regress a client into a past life and these sessions are each spaced one week apart. The client is required to practice a self-hypnosis technique at home every day, so that they can go deeper when they arrive for their regression.

Some hypnotherapists are happy to regress clients into past lives in the first session, but I'm somewhat unsure about the results. If the client is not deep enough in hypnosis, they'll be imagining their past lives and clients can probably do that at home without spending any money, time or effort.

I use a lake as a metaphor for the conscious and subconscious minds. Although you may row your boat out to the centre of the lake, you are unaware of what lies at the bottom. If you scoop some water out of the lake with your hands, it will come from the top of the lake. This can be likened to the surface memories, such as your name, address, and what you ate for lunch yesterday.

If you take a bucket and send it deeper into the lake, retrieving water from several feet down, this can be likened to deeper memories, such as where you went to school and the house you grew up in as a teenager. Accessing such memories requires that you enter a medium depth of hypnosis.

If you were to don diving gear and descend to the bottom of the lake, retrieving water from there to view, it would be as though you have accessed your deepest memories. Such memories include details from infancy, birth and previous lives. This requires a deep hypnotic state to accurately access these memories while awake. They can be accessed during sleep through dreams, but are not necessarily recalled clearly in the waking state.

Once you have retrieved memories from infancy or from past lives and examined them closely, they will start to fade from your conscious mind. Like an object retrieved from a lake's bed and then dropped into the lake again, past life memories slowly return to deep within your subconscious mind just as the object returns to the bottom of the lake.

3. Rebirthing

Rebirthing is a connected breathing technique and is a powerful tool for accessing past lives. Popular in the 1980s and 1990s, it has the advantage of triggering the subject directly into past lives without the need for preparatory sessions.

The downside of rebirthing is that if the client resists what she is experiencing, she can experience a state of temporary paralysis of her hands and feet. If her resistance continues, this paralysis can extend to the arms and legs. It's easy to state that you will not resist, but when faced with overwhelming emotional and physical pain, it is very hard not to resist. An example of resistance occurred with Boyd, who used rebirthing to access his past lives.

During one session, he re-experienced a lifetime involving his present-life father. They were friends, and both were soldiers. They fought side by side through many battles and grew very close. One day when they were out on their own, Boyd's friend attacked him and plunged a sword into his heart. As Boyd lay there, betrayed and dying, his friend looked down on him and smiled, telling him that he was planning to take Boyd's partner for himself after Boyd's death.

With all the energy he could muster, Boyd resisted the images and feelings of the death on the ground beneath his former friend and in the session he started to experience paralysis of the hands and feet. Such was his resistance that Boyd spent more than three hours locked in paralysis of the arms and legs, feeling the pain of the betrayal and his slow descent into death. He said that he felt bruised and shattered for days after the session, but that it was a worthwhile experience as it explained why he had difficulty trusting his present-life father.

Rebirthing is best done under supervision of an experienced practitioner and is not recommended for those with heart problems.

4. Meditation

With the aid of specific meditations, you can access your past lives easily and at a time that suits you. Spirit guide meditations are beneficial, as you can ask what lesson is contained within a situation, without having to go full-tilt into the feelings.

Some people prefer the heady emotions that accompany each past-life experience. 'Where would we be without a bit of kicking and screaming?' is how one friend puts it and perhaps he's right. It can become addictive, especially if your present life is somewhat routine and safe. Immersing yourself into an assignment where you know that you will die and yet return to the room where you started can be just the adventure some of us crave.

Meditation is useful for when you are experiencing frustration in your present-day life and you need to know why. You can meditate and ask your spirit guides to show you the lessons contained in the present circumstances. Sometimes to illustrate your lessons they take you back to past lives to show you where you have interacted with particular people and how those interactions ended. (For more information on meditation procedures see *A Secret Door to the Universe*, Simon & Schuster Australia, 1999)

The drawbacks with meditation include poor meditation sessions resulting in imagined results and scrappy information. Like poor radio reception, a distracted meditation can leave you with feelings of frustration and limited clear information about your past lives.

Poor meditations can occur any time, just as good, deep clear meditations can be achieved unexpectedly. I was surprised at the depth of a meditation one night after three days tending to my five-year-old boy, who had a bad bout of asthma. I'd been up five times the first night, six times the second and three times on the third night to give him medication and to comfort him. When I fell into bed on the fourth night, I was exhausted but physically wound up and mentally alert from listening out for him wheezing in the next room.

Deciding to take a few minutes to meditate to help me unwind, I fell deep into meditation and was taken back immediately to a past life where my son and I were close friends and this time he was tending to me. I was shown that my actions of the past few nights were only mirroring his actions of many years ago. After this meditation, it was easier for me to get out of bed to attend to him.

Not all soul-mate relationships run as smoothly, however, because past-life patterns can emerge that need to be resolved. These include issues of abandonment, as experienced by another couple, Ella and Luke.

Luke had never been possessive of his partners until he met Ella. After three years she was being driven insane by his fear that she was about to leave him forever. During a past-life regression, Ella discovered that in a former life they had been a couple and that she had been a male in that lifetime. Soon after they had met in that life, Ella had been called away to war and had died in battle, leaving his partner distraught with grief. As the female partner in that lifetime, Luke had died during childbirth after a pregnancy plagued with bouts of deep depression.

This unresolved issue of abandonment resurfaced in this lifetime, despite continuing evidence that Ella was here to stay. After much encouragement, Ella convinced Luke to undergo counselling and he was able to resolve his past life-issue of abandonment.

Pursuing a love relationship with a soul mate can be both an exhilarating and frustrating experience, but few people who have done so seem to regret it. Depths of love and understanding are available in soul-mate relationships that can inspire the soul or strike terror into the hearts of those presented with such opportunities.

When you look across a crowded room and time stands still as your soul recognises someone from the past, will you be ready for the spiritual opportunity that love offers you? Or will you stumble into the arms of an opportunity, only half awake to the realisation that fate is at hand, guiding you towards your spiritual destination?

Chapter Three

FINDING YOUR LESSONS TOGETHER

❧

DETERMINING WHAT LESSONS YOU HAVE TO MASTER THIS TIME AROUND CAN BE DIFFICULT, AS LESSONS OFTEN APPEAR ONLY AS YOU ARE READY TO LEARN THEM. In some cases, if you knew what mountains you had to climb together, you might choose to give up before you started the friendship. Once the bonds of friendship are in place, however, it is more difficult to release the friendship, so you are more likely to carry things through until you complete the issues and learn the lessons together.

Developing a strong sense of personal awareness can help in determining the lessons involved with soul mates, as these lessons are often within the grasp of your conscious awareness when you first meet. Because of circumstances and life's demands, you may not recognise these lessons again until they appear in a more concrete form. Also, if, when you meet, you are holding a drink in one hand and trying to sing in key, your awareness is focused upon the tasks at hand and you are less likely to notice the lesson just beneath your conscious awareness.

A clairvoyant reading can help you to fathom the lessons in a soul-mate friendship or love relationship, if the clairvoyant is accurate. I caution against trusting someone who is very vague or who states cliches such as 'your lesson is to learn unconditional love'. I'm perhaps cynical about unconditional love, believing that it only exists between parents and children, and even then not as much as it could exist. The love between emotionally healthy parents and their children recognises the dependence children have on their parents and the responsibilities involved in being a role model for the growing child. As adults, we form friendships and love relationships to meet our own needs and not necessarily those of our partner, so at times there is precious little that is unconditional about these relationships.

A good clairvoyant reading will highlight the past issues and present circumstances before telling you about the lessons ahead of you both. You already know the past issues (in this lifetime) and the present circumstances, so if the clairvoyant is wrong on those counts, you can dismiss any further information he or she gives you. If they are correct on those counts, however, it's likely that you'll receive valuable information about your spiritual lessons within your soul-mate friendship.

Counselling can highlight the lessons as they surface in the form of issues between the two of you. If these issues are repetitive, then you can see the lesson lain out before you. Consulting a counsellor is usually a choice made when the issues have already surfaced, and not at the beginning of a soul-mates friendship or relationship.

Meditation is another powerful way to illuminate the lessons in a soul-mate friendship or love relationship, and to do this you need to be able to reach a deep and undisturbed meditative state. If your meditation is light or disturbed, you risk imagining the lessons involved and being no closer to the truth after your efforts.

In a deep meditation you can ask yourself what the lesson is in a particular soul-mates relationship or you can ask your spirit guides. Either way, it is recommended that you only ask one question at a sitting, so that you can retrieve clear information that you will recall after you have concluded your meditation. A common mistake is to take a long list of questions into a single meditation and return confused and none the wiser. If you can achieve one deep meditation, you can achieve another. One clear, well-worded question per meditation can give you all the information you require for that period of time.

An example of asking too many questions occurred during a clairvoyant reading recently. Despite being told that the reading only covered the next two years, the client pressed me to tell her more and more about long-term events. When I told her that she was likely to outlive her husband by 13 years, she was shocked. She had heard something she was unprepared to hear, and it couldn't be taken back. Before you ask about long-term lessons within your soul-mate relationships, ask yourself if you are prepared to have your questions answered negatively. Are you prepared to deal with shocking or disappointing news?

It is possible that your present soul-mate friendship stems from a past-life conflict, and that your friend this lifetime was a past-life enemy. Not all soul-mate friendships end well, especially where there has been conflict in previous interactions.

I have seen soul-mate friendships that ended in one friend attempting to annihilate the other over what appeared to be a trivial matter, but which was, in fact, a repeat of a past-life source of great pain to the friend who lashed out. If you have abandoned a friend or partner in a past life and you do so again in this one, it is possible that the present abandonment might trigger all those past-life feelings of loss, anguish and betrayal. The person may act upon all of the residual feelings, behaving in a way that seems out of proportion to the current circumstances.

Dreams offer another way to identify your underlying spiritual lessons within a soul-mate relationship, and recording your dreams in a dream diary or even a pad beside the bed (for dreams to be written up first thing in the morning) is a powerful method for some people. The longer you record your dreams, the more likely your subconscious mind will be able to give you the details you seek about your soul-mate relationship lessons. This technique is better suited to those with patience, as initial results can be some time coming.

Chapter Four

WHAT SORT OF RELATIONSHIP DO YOU CREATE?

❧

The Boat

AS A METAPHOR FOR LOVE RELATIONSHIPS, A BOAT SAILING UPON THE SEA IS USEFUL. The size and strength of the boat signifies the strength of the relationship and the water upon which it floats represents the emotional issues that we face in love relationships. Some days the sea appears to be awash with craft, sailing close to one another, while other days you may stare searchingly out to sea and not spy one boat. Calm waters may give way to turbulent seas within hours, just as a stable relationship may encounter emotionally charged issues at short notice.

Imagine that one day you set sail alone on a 32-foot boat, ready for an afternoon's adventure. In a few hours, the shoreline is disappearing and you are having a fabulous day. The strong sun and the steady winds serve to take you a long way from anyone.

A storm approaches suddenly and your boat is tossed like a toy upon the enormous swell. The sky darkens and visibility is less than five feet in front of you with rain sheeting down at a 45-degree angle, directly into your face. You are knocked unconscious as the boat breaks up and you are washed ashore a small tropical island. You awaken in the dark, confused and alone, and you huddle beneath some trees for protection.

In the morning you survey your surroundings, finding few remnants of your boat and realising that you are indeed alone. You collect some firewood in order to signal the next passing vessel and you stare out toward the horizon in hope of an early rescue. The days stretch into weeks and the weeks soon become months. Every day the horizon is your first and your last visual focus, as you are desperate to be rescued from your loneliness.

Seven years, three months, two weeks and five days pass and not one boat is seen. Several times you feel that you have glimpsed a ship, only to find that you were mistaken. You have landed upon one of more than 1,600 islands in the South Pacific and you now know what it feels like to be truly alone.

After lunch one afternoon, you are sitting on the sand when your peripheral vision is alerted to a shape on the horizon. Is it a boat? Could this be the end of your predicament?

You set the firewood ablaze to signal to the occupants of the vessel and an enormous cargo ship moves slowly towards you. The crew manoeuvres it as close to the island as possible, and the captain picks up a loudhailer to speak to you. He explains that as he is in these waters illegally, he cannot collect you. Nor can he tell anyone that he has seen you, without incriminating himself. However, he offers to send one crew member to visit you for two weeks. In two weeks they'll return from their destination and collect the crew member, but you must remain behind.

He offers you a choice:

1. Allow a crew member to visit you for two weeks, and then that person will re-board the ship to return from whence they came.

2. Refuse the visitor and watch them sail away again.

What do you choose?

As you ponder this, it occurs to you that the crew member may be a man or a woman. They may not speak your language and they may not share any of your interests. On the other hand, they may offer you ideas, conversations and discussions that you would otherwise never have without their visit. You realise that if you say yes, you'll start to miss the visitor as soon as they set foot on your island. From the moment of their arrival, their departure will be looming.

You are confused. You ask if there is any way that you can accompany them back to a destination, any populated destination, but the captain refuses. He apologises that he has nothing more to offer you than one visitor for two weeks. He offers you ten minutes in which to decide.

Is this very different to life and to love relationships? We are born and we land on our island. Someone approaches us with love and we have to decide if we want what they are offering for as long as they offer it to us, if we want them to be with us forever, or not at all.

I have told this story and put this question to hundreds of people, almost always receiving one of two answers:

1. Yes, tell them to come for the two weeks.
2. No, tell them not to come unless they can come forever or I can accompany them home.

I point out that even if you fall in love only once in your lifetime and you marry your desired partner, they may be called from this life before you. You have no choice in how many years are allotted you this lifetime, and rarely do both partners pass away at the same time.

A few times I have received another answer. This answer involves saying 'yes' to the visitor and then killing them when they arrive. When the cargo ship arrives two weeks later, you return to it dressed in their clothes.

After ten years of asking this question, a close friend came to me a few days after I had asked her, with what I consider to be the perfect answer. She said: 'I'd say yes to the visitor and together we would spend the two weeks building a boat for me to sail away in after the visitor had left.' It sounded so clear and so perfect.

In effect, she was saying that each relationship builds a boat for each partner to sail, and if the relationship ends, the partner can sail away safely. So what sort of boat are you building right now? Is it a flimsy, rot-ridden dinghy? Does it have oars? Is it carefully polished and lovingly crafted or hastily assembled and crudely shaped?

In a recent workshop on soul mates, I asked the students what sort of boat they were building and asked them to go out and purchase a painting or a photo of the boat of their choice, to remind them that they are indeed in the business of boat building.

If you have to set to sea for an unseen destination, it might as well be in the boat of your preference, don't you think?

Exercise

1. Take a few minutes to complete this exercise. You'll need a pen and a pad to help you to review you first love relationship.
2. What sort of boat did you build together in your first major love relationship? (How did it shape your life attitudes?)
3. List what you sailed away from that relationship carrying? List both the positive and the negative things. Did your boat have too much ballast? Were there too many negative attitudes and emotions weighing you down as you sailed away or did you set a clear course towards your next relationship?
List Positive things. List negative things.
4. Now examine your second important love relationship. What sort of boat did you build together?
5. Did you apply yourselves equally to the task at hand or did one of you build while the other rested?
6. Did you sail away from that first love relationship towards your second relationship or did you bump into another boat and leap from deck to deck without a backward glance?

By examining your past love relationships you may notice a pattern of boats. Perhaps you are building rowing boats when you really desire a sloop?

7. Now describe what sort of boat (or life attitudes) you are presently building, if you are building one at this stage in your life.

Complete this exercise before proceeding with the next chapter.

Chapter Five

SOUL MATES
AS FRIENDS

❧

ALTHOUGH THE TERM 'SOUL MATE' IS OFTEN USED TO
DESCRIBE A LOVE RELATIONSHIP PARTNER, SOUL MATES
CAN APPEAR IN YOUR LIFE AS FRIENDS. Being soul mates
doesn't mean that you have to have a sexual relationship, as many
lessons can be learned through other means. A business venture
with a partner, or a long-term friendship, can sometimes offer you
the opportunities to learn your spiritual lessons together.

An example of a soul-mate friendship occurred with Margaret.
She was sharing an old terraced house in a Sydney suburb in the
early 1980s with Nicole, and she described meeting a soul mate
by chance.

Nicole was standing outside the back gate flirting with one of
the neighbours in the lane while Margaret washed her clothes.
Another neighbour, Heather, was transferring topsoil from the
back of a truck to her garden via the lane. The squeaking wheel of
the barrow was heard echoing down the lane as Heather passed

with each load, and Nicole and Brent nodded each time she passed them.

As Margaret hung out a pair of sheets she looked up at the sound of Heather's barrow and their eyes met. They smiled to one another and Margaret felt compelled to follow Heather into her small garden to speak with her. An hour later they were immersed in shovelling and raking the topsoil as though they had been friends for years.

More than 15 years later, they are still firm friends and they share an intuitive link with one another, allowing each person to know when the other needs help or support. Several times Heather has phoned Margaret at times when Margaret desperately needed help and support, and Margaret has intuitively known when Heather needed help. Although they live far apart now, they have a deep friendship which, due to its intense beginnings, has the hallmarks of a past-life friendship.

Soul-mate friendships can also be the result of a soul-mate love relationship that has ended. Often, if the karma involved between the couple is not complete, then a friendship can continue the lessons after the love relationship has concluded.

After my own marriage concluded, I remained friends with my former wife as we had only five years (of marriage) to complete our karma together. Having a child continues the karma but that won't necessarily call us back together in another lifetime.

That feeling of recognition at meeting a soul mate can occur in many ways. I recall one such meeting occurring over a round of margaritas while some friends were singing heartily around my piano one evening. As Renee sat playing the piano, Darryl took a break from the saxophone to sing along in harmony. At the end of the song they laughed heartily at all of their mistakes and although they had only met that evening, they appeared to have been lifelong friends. Their friendship was intense and instant, and, after that night, their lives have been as much in harmony as they were when singing around the piano.

Deep feelings of trust and familiarity often accompany a meeting of a soul mate where there have been positive experiences shared in past lives together. More often, however, there are mixed feelings, as even positive past lives are mixed with difficult times or betrayals between yourself and your new-found soul mate. It stands to reason that not all of your past times shared ended smoothly, so there are likely to be unresolved issues. That doesn't mean that there will be great pain or suffering in your friendship this time around, but that the issues need to resurface to be healed. When the outstanding issues have been resolved, you can decide whether to continue the friendship or release it.

Another example of the unexpected benefits of a soul-mates friendship occurred with Albert, a wealthy businessman, and Marina, who was unable to work after a serious car accident. Her twisted form made most people glance away when she looked up and she spent her days in social isolation. Albert often noticed Marina around the local mall when he was out getting a sandwich for lunch or heading for the bank, and he felt the urge to assist her financially. At first he smiled and said hello as he passed and in time Marina warmed to him. Her twisted body made it hard for her to walk any distance, and she spent most of her days sitting on a wooden bench seat under a tree in the mall. One afternoon Albert was negotiating his car through traffic in a downpour when he noticed Marina slowly walking home in the rain. He offered her a ride and when she recognised him, she smiled and accepted.

Soon Albert was helping Marina with her weekly shopping and occasionally she visited Albert and his wife for dinner. Albert described it as 'Giving back a little of what life has given me', and he was a visible example of the saying 'Charity begins at home'. When I questioned him more closely he couldn't explain why he singled out Marina for help. 'I just sensed that I had to help this girl. It was as though God showed her to me and it was up to me to respond or to ignore her,' he said and shrugged. Over the next two years they became firm friends and I often saw Albert's huge frame towering above Marina's twisted body as he carried her bags back to his car, before driving her home.

Both Albert and Marina seemed to grow from their friendship

and Marina was able to help Albert in return one afternoon when she found him slumped in the front seat of his car as it stood in the local shopping centre car park. At first Marina thought that Albert was on the phone, then thought he was asleep, but a feeling within her alerted her to the fact that something was wrong. She staggered to a shop to summon help and it turned out that Albert had suffered a stroke. It was only because Marina had recognised Albert's expensive car in the car park and summoned help that he was hospitalised in time.

Sometimes soul-mate friendships offer you someone whom you can trust in times of crisis, and in other cases such friendships offer you the chance to repay a past-life debt in the kindest way imaginable.

Past lives shared with family members

Surprisingly, present-life family members have often shared past lives together. Being born in the same family is one way to ensure you have an opportunity to master any outstanding lessons or to spend more time together.

Aside from the usual issues such as sibling rivalry, same-family soul mates can display their issues openly as small children, or they'll appear between parents and children.

When I held my son a few minutes after he was born, I knew that we had been together before and that we'd been equals and friends. It was good karma returning to me in the form of someone who was to rely upon me to guide him into adulthood.

Even as a seven-year-old, he can't wait to be as big as me again, because he seems to recall our being equal in the past and he wants that relationship back. I gently remind him that I'm the father and he's the child this time, only to receive a look that says 'What would you know?'

Family soul mates are not always easy relationships, as the following example illustrates. Years ago, I was using hypnosis to regress a client back to the first moments of this lifetime and she detailed an unusual situation. The nurse handed her to her mother, who studied her newborn carefully. Slowly a look of fear came over her mother's face and my client described the accompanying energy as saying, 'It's you. Oh no, it's you again.' Her mother recognised her energy as someone who had caused her pain somewhere in the past. As an adult, the client has a tense relationship with her mother, and if they have been past-life enemies, they appear not to have made too much progress towards resolution in this lifetime.

Another client, Ryan, chose hypnosis regression into past lives as a way to discover why, as a child, he was so badly treated by his father. Ryan's father was continuously cruel to him, before sending him interstate to a boarding school. His sister, however, was very well treated by her father, who indulged her every whim.

The past-life regression highlighted a competition between Ryan and his father for a woman's affection. Ryan had triumphed and his father had become embittered in that lifetime as a result of being denied the woman he desired.

I asked Ryan if he recognised the energy of the woman from that lifetime in the present life. A look of shock came over him and he nodded. It was his younger sister. The three of them had returned together in a family to resolve the karma, only this time he was the one excluded. Ryan's father was still attempting to win the affections of a person who had rejected him previously, only this time she was his daughter.

Armed with this knowledge, Ryan was able to realise that his father's actions were probably based on unconscious feelings and desires from a past life. This did not diminish his grief at the treatment from his father, but it gave Ryan a better perspective from which to assess the situation.

In the same way that your thoughts, desires and actions from past lives are affecting this life, your actions in this life can affect subsequent lifetimes. I see partners and family members continuously setting themselves up for pain and, by their current actions, creating situations that will demand resolution in the future.

Such situations are not hard to find. At the death of a family member (especially a parent), siblings can become ruthless in their pursuit of the spoils of the efforts of a lifetime of hard work. An example of this occurred with Laura, who consulted me regarding a legal challenge to her father's will.

A wealthy man, her father had financially supported Laura on many occasions during his life, when she wanted to purchase a business, when the business failed and she needed two million dollars to repay creditors; and when she wanted to start another business with her new husband. When the time came to make his last will and testament, Laura's father decided that he had supported her enough financially throughout her life, and that it was now her husband's turn to do so. To this end he left her $100,000, and the remaining $40 million he spread among his nieces and nephews.

Laura consulted me to see if a legal challenge would lead her to a greater share of his estate but I saw that he was a careful man — he'd tied up his estate in four different ways to ensure that there could be no successful legal challenge to his final wishes. The family was embittered by the legal wrangling, and Laura had already spent close to $50,000 in legal fees, to no end.

I stressed to Laura that she had already received more than $5 million from her father throughout his life and that no member of his extended family was to receive as much from his estate, but she wouldn't be placated. Although his actions seemed well founded, Laura's father had started a row that is likely to last for several generations.

Past-life enemies make for uncomfortable siblings, at least until the past-life issues have been resolved. It is entirely possible that growing up with certain people may be enough to make you dislike them for life, but I've seen relationships between family members that were so entrenched in their antipathy to one another that it could not be dismissed as sibling rivalry.

Chapter Six

HOW MANY SOUL MATES IN THIS LIFETIME?

❧

THE DAYS OF HAVING ONE LOVE RELATIONSHIP FOR LIFE ARE NOW ALL BUT OVER. Where once, life expectancy was around 35 years and women started families in their teenage years, we now have more opportunities and choices than ever before. Improvements in hygiene, sources of food and medicine mean that most of us don't have to live in survival mode and with the constant fear of death. With our survival taken care of, we can focus upon less obvious things, such as our spiritual purpose, our friendships and our love relationships. Because we live longer, we have the opportunity to progress more spiritually.

This means that where a lifelong relationship may once have started when you were 16 years old and concluded with your death at 35, some of us have not yet met our life partner by 35, or we may be in the first of several long relationships. It is possible now to have several soul-mate love relationship opportunities in one lifetime, with each relationship offering you a chance to master a different lesson. This is not to suggest that you are obliged to pursue each and every soul mate opportunity, or that you need to pursue them as love relationships. If you are already in a love relationship to which you are committed, it is possible to have a friendship with someone who is offering you a soul mate opportunity.

In some cases of soul mates meeting again, they have had such a good time in a past life that they energetically agreed to reunite at another time. When we meet in this lifetime, however, circumstances may prevent us from pursuing a love relationship, so we honour our agreement to meet and then we part again.

Limiting circumstances in this lifetime might include:

- an age difference of 40 years or more;
- being born into the same family;
- being of the same gender and one or both persons unwilling to pursue a same-gender love relationship;
- one or both soul mates choosing a life of celibacy;
- one partner already has a relationship or family that they cannot abandon;
- one partner is terrified of the power of the love they feel for the other and avoids the opportunity for a love relationship; or
- cultural or religious differences that prevent a love relationship.

A friend of mine, Damien, met a past-life partner and was overwhelmed by the power of the love they felt for one another. He described it as being enveloped by an incredible stillness when they were together, where all needs evaporated and only love existed.

I asked him why he didn't pursue it and he grew heavy with regret and sighed.

'I was ambitious, and being with Adele cured me of my ambitions. When I was with her, I was content just to be alive. In time I grew scared that if we stayed together, I'd never achieve my goals. In effect, I traded my ambitions for a life of fulfilment.'

'And have you kept in touch with Adele?'

'Yes, we're still good friends. She married another man and they have three children. She's very happy and he seems content too. I sometimes look at him and see the life I might have chosen.'

It seemed strange to me that a man might trade a soul-mate love relationship for career ambitions, until I realised that Damien wanted to achieve something in his career because he felt that with achievement, he had something worthwhile to offer a potential partner. He couldn't see that Adele loved him for who he was and not what he was achieving.

After Damien told me this, I started looking to see if other people also avoided opportunities for love and I was surprised. The more I searched the more I found men and women running away from the one thing that they sought most – love. What usually fuelled their running away was ambition.

Ambition can isolate us from one another, as it involves competition with others for the available opportunities. For a time, two partners can share an ambition, but ultimately career ambitions often separate them. Having observed this, I returned to Damien to ask him some questions.

'When you have achieved your ambitions, and you are successful, who will you share it all with?' I asked him. He thought about this for a few minutes before speaking.

'I always imagined that along the way I'd meet a girl and we'd tread the path together, but it seems that I've continued to tread the path and girls have come and gone.'

'Have they had their own paths to tread?'

'Some of them. Others just grew tired of me living and breathing my goals. It's very lonely reaching for such difficult goals.'

'I'm sure it is. Is it even more difficult knowing that you had a deep and lasting opportunity with Adele but that you left it behind?'

'Yes and no. I miss her deeply sometimes, especially when we talk on the phone. She has this softness that gets right under my guard and I can't hide my feelings from her. But then, after I've hung up the phone, I remind myself that she is happy living a simple life in a small, rundown house in the country whereas I need the city for my life and for my work.'

'So your head accepts that you need to achieve certain goals, but how about your heart?'

'It's hard sometimes, especially when I feel alone and that no-one truly understands me. Adele knew me well. Very well. In fact, within two weeks of meeting me she knew me right down to the cells of each and every part of me. When someone knows you that well, there is no escape from the softness, the tenderness, which melted my ambitions. What use was I to anyone when I was blissfully happy?'

I couldn't believe that I was hearing this.

'Are you saying that it was because you felt too loved and understood by Adele that you left her?' I asked him.

'Okay, I admit it. I ran away. I ran away from too much love. You don't understand. All of my life so far, I've longed to be loved and understood, just like anyone. But when you receive what you've longed for, what else is there after that? I knew that it would all be a downhill slide after Adele, so I chose to achieve those things in career that I wanted, with the hope that another Adele exists out there for me when I am older.'

'And what if there isn't another soul mate out there for you? What if you die from career-related stress in the meantime?'

'That's a risk I'm prepared to take. It's okay for you. You don't know what it's like to have all of your deepest fears accepted by someone else, and all of your inner desires melt because you are already fulfilled just by being near your soul mate. It sounds like heaven but it's hell. It's hell because all those ambitions I held onto in order to make my life seem worthwhile faded away into dust. I was terrified that such a deep love might swallow me whole.'

'How did Adele's love swallow you whole?'

'One afternoon we were lying on the bed together and she draped one arm across my stomach. As I lay there, I could feel her love for me radiating from her arm and filling me with joy. We lay there for about 30 minutes and it was pure bliss. I could become addicted to that level of bliss very easily. I decided afterwards that our relationship was stealing my ambitions.'

'I see it differently. I think that your ambitions were stealing your chance to love and be loved by someone special.' He nodded, realising that this was partly true.

Most of us will have several opportunities for soul-mate love relationships and friendships in addition to the soul mates we have in family members and friends. Whether we accept these opportunities is entirely up to us. I was speaking with a friend named Sasha recently, who described three soul-mate love relationships she has experienced. The first, her husband Dennis, taught her the value of practical application of plans, as he was a disciplined man who had his feet planted firmly on the ground. As Sasha spoke, I could see that she greatly admired him.

The second, Peter, was so lost in his life that Sasha determined to find her spiritual purpose through meditation and through reading all the spiritual books she could get her hands on. Peter is still lost, but their relationship was enough to open Sasha's eyes to what life offered to those who live in the moment.

The third was Enzo, whose confidence in life's possibilities inspired Sasha to reach for goals she previously felt were unattainable. Enzo simply decided what he wanted and set about bringing his plans into reality. He was a creative man, being an artist and a musician, and was successful in many of his ventures. Even as she spoke, Sasha was passionate about how much of an inspiration Enzo had been to her and how he had unlocked potential within her that no-one else had even seen.

'I've been very lucky really,' she said to me over a cup of tea one afternoon. 'I've had three fabulous relationships, oh, and some time-wasters too, don't get me wrong. Do you think it's selfish of me to expect another soul-mate relationship after all that I've had?'

'Just the one more?' I asked teasingly.

'Well if it's a good, long one yes. If not, then it would be nice to have a few more. I'll be a little old lady, standing in the supermarket, flirting with someone who's desperately clinging to his trolley for stability while I scour the contents of his trolley to see if we have food tastes in common. The right coffee and a good brand of chocolate biscuits and I'm in.'

'You're easily pleased if the right brand of chocolate biscuits confirms a past-life connection,' I laughed.

Just because you may have another opportunity for a soul-mate love relationship, doesn't mean that you can throw away current opportunities, as nothing is guaranteed. Your next opportunity may arrive a week after you are buried.

Chapter Seven

MEETING SOUL MATES IN DREAMS

SOMETIMES DUE TO LOCATION, WE NEVER MEET CERTAIN SOUL MATES IN THE PHYSICAL SENSE. Instead we meet one another in dreams at night, travelling together astrally and learning our lessons in other dimensions. We may or may not recall such events upon awakening.

You can train yourself to recall many of your astral experiences, which may highlight the lessons you are learning during sleep. Some simple techniques are listed below.

Dream recall techniques

1. Keep a pen and a pad beside the bed so that you can write down what you recall soon after awakening. Many dreams are remembered soon after awakening but are forgotten within hours due to the conscious concerns you have in your daily life.

2. You need to tell your subconscious mind that you want to recall your dreams, and to do this you need to access your subconscious mind when it is most open to suggestions. Your subconscious mind is most open to suggestions when you are in meditation, in a hypnotic state, or as you fall asleep.

3 When we fall asleep at night, most of us have physical positions we assume as we drift off into sleep. Many people turn over onto one side and when they do this, they soon drift away from consciousness. If you turn over, this is the time to tell yourself the following: 'Tonight I'll dream and tomorrow I'll awaken remembering all of my dreams easily and vividly. I will remember my dreams all day tomorrow.' Then simply allow yourself to drift off to sleep. Don't make a big production out of it. Simply tell yourself that you'll remember your dreams in the morning upon awakening.

4. Make up a tape recording of your own voice telling yourself that you'll recall your dreams easily and clearly upon awakening in the morning. State what you want (and not what you don't want) as the subconscious mind takes suggestions literally. Be literal. If you consider yourself talking to a child, you'd be more effective in telling them to be safe on the roads instead of telling them not to get themselves run over by a car.

5. Upon awakening, spend five to 10 minutes recalling your dreams before you start your daily routines.

This simple technique may take a few days or even weeks to start achieving the results you desire, yet with practice it works. I've seen clients who have used these techniques to recall enough dreams to fill several dream diaries over the years. In turn, they have gained great insights into themselves and their lives.

One example of meeting a soul mate in dreams occurred with a friend who dreamed of travel experiences he shared with a man in Asia every night for almost six weeks. Through dreams he'd meet this man who was meditating at the time of the shared experience. After the initial six weeks, all dream contact stopped for almost a year. When contact resumed, my friend's soul mate explained that he'd given up meditation at that time due to changed life circumstances. His new meditation time occurred when my friend was awake, and no subconscious contact was made.

Another friend often described her meditation experiences with her spiritual master in India. While living in London, she meditated in order to ask her master's advice on important matters and in her meditations he'd answer her clearly. Her spiritual master was considered her living master, responsible for her spiritual advancement in this lifetime.

Don't expect to spend your every sleeping moment travelling the astral plane in search of living and non-living soul mates, as you'll probably only awaken tired and unrefreshed from a long sleep. Brief sojourns into the ethereal worlds in search of confirmation that someone you loved, or still love, exists out there with a shared history do occur. From time to time you may be faced with an enormous spiritual challenge in your life that requires support or a reminder (through dreams) that you have faced similar challenges in previous times and succeeded.

At other times it may be necessary for you to travel to meet a past-life partner or friend in order to receive some information relevant to your current spiritual path. I am aware of cases where someone is faced with an enormous burden, and they receive a visit from a soul mate who has been with them this lifetime but who is deceased. The visit is to give them strength to face the burdens.

In one case, a friend named Grace, whose husband David had died in a car accident, received such a visit. Two years after his death, David visited Grace three nights in a row during her sleep. He repeatedly told her that positive changes were just around the corner for her. Grace had been sliding into depression, partly from exhaustion with the two children, and partly from not having grieved properly when David died. His visits were of great comfort to Grace, whose life did improve shortly after the dreams. Grace met a new partner three months later who helped her to gradually walk back into life.

When your current soul mates are away from you (interstate or overseas), they may visit you in your dreams, depending upon the time zones in which each of you sleep. An example of this occurred recently with my young son who was overseas on holiday in Europe. He must have fallen asleep during the day (night-time in Australia) for he came to me in a dream one night. He told me that he was tired of being away and that he wanted to come home. We laughed and talked for awhile and I told him that I was eagerly awaiting his return. Our meeting still had dream-like qualities, yet such meetings are usually characterised by a sharpness and a sense of continuity that many dreams don't have. You are also more likely to recall meetings with soul mates in the dream state than regular dreams, provided you are experiencing a normal, natural healthy sleep. If you are using sleeping tablets or drinking alcohol, these substances may impair your recollection of dreams and astral experiences during sleep.

Some soul mates are met only through dreams in this lifetime, whereas other soul mates with whom you've shared time but who are not presently in your life, may visit you from time to time in dreams to see how you are, or to update you with news about their current life circumstances. A former partner of mine appeared in my dreams several times and although I was too busy to remember the exact content of our conversations, I awoke thinking of her and wondering about her health. I felt that something was wrong with her back and a week after the first dream I phoned her. When I asked her about her health and particularly her back, she gasped and explained that her father had just been diagnosed with cancer which was located in the spinal vertebrae.

She had visited me in a dream to explain her father's health and how it was affecting her. As I knew her father, she thought that I'd want to know the bad news. Although we had not been together for over ten years, time didn't matter, as it doesn't with soul mates. Had I been less preoccupied with my own life and its deadlines, I might have recalled the dream (her astral visit to me) more clearly and phoned her earlier.

Chapter Eight

SAME-GENDER
SOUL MATES

❧

A S WE EXPERIENCE SUCCESSIVE LIVES AS DIFFERENT GENDERS, IT STANDS TO REASON THAT WE'LL HAVE SPENT TIME WITH SOUL MATES WHO ARE WOMEN NOW BUT WHO WERE MEN WHEN WE KNEW THEM AND VICE VERSA. Same-gender soul mates appear both in friendships and in love relationships, as gender has only a limited impact upon the lessons involved. An example of a same-gender soul-mate love relationship occurred with Scott, who met his soul mate, Max, across a crowded bar one night.

It was the first time 19-year-old Scott had ventured into a gay bar and he stood close to the open fire, nervously sipping his orange juice, trying to avoid eye contact with the other patrons. After an hour he had forgotten the frosty night outside and traded his orange juice for a Vodka and orange.

The butterflies in his stomach had long given way to moths and he looked up to see an old acquaintance from school standing with one hand on the mantle. They engaged in a light conversation and as they spoke, Scott glanced around the room. He was surprised to find that he recognised at least nine other people he knew from school days and he started to relax slightly.

After another 15 minutes of light conversation, Scott glanced around the room again and stopped when his eyes met Max. All sounds in the room fell away and time slowed to an immeasurable pace as they stood, transfixed by one another. The shyness Scott had been feeling disappeared and he knew that he had to speak with Max, if only for a moment. As Max was speaking with another of Scott's school acquaintances, Scott saw his way into their conversation.

Before he could move towards them, however, he had to recall the name of the man beside Max. His mind raced through a long list of names from the likely to the distinctly absurd, but he couldn't recall the name. He'd have to chance it. Taking a deep breath, Scott strode over to Max and his friend as he thought of what he might say when he arrived. He needn't have worried, as Max spoke first.

'What took you so long?' he asked Scott.

'What?'

'What took you so long to notice me here?'

'I don't know. I'm nervous, I guess,' stammered Scott.

'I felt you in the room the moment I arrived. In fact, I had to walk around the room to find out why my radar was going off,' laughed Max.

Max knew from the moment he entered the crowded room that there was someone that he had to meet that night, whereas Scott's nervousness probably prevented him from knowing the same thing. They started a relationship and were together for five years. In that time Max introduced Scott to spiritual development and together they discovered their unfinished lessons. After their relationship concluded, they remained friends, as they were already friends before they met again this lifetime, by the fire in a hotel on a frosty night.

Gender may have some bearing upon how we learn our lessons in a love relationship but relationships are relationships, regardless of the genders of the partners involved. If life gives us an opportunity to resolve some karma, to learn valuable lessons and to love and be loved in return, why would we choose to refuse such an opportunity? (See Chapter 10, 'Saying 'No' to a Soul-Mate Opportunity'.)

An example of life offering an opportunity for spiritual development through a same-gender love relationship occurred with Karen, who was a regular client of mine. As she shuffled the tarot cards, I heard a voice within me state: 'Be careful what you say today as circumstances are different now.'

I was vigilant as I scanned the cards she had selected for a love relationship question, and there it was. Although she had always asked about men in the past, she was asking about a woman that day. I described the woman and Karen was in tears, explaining that although she had tried to resist a love relationship, she felt drawn to this woman. She described feeling more alive than ever before, and although the woman concerned was not that keen to pursue a love relationship together, Karen felt this was to be a special interaction and an opportunity to reach previously hidden depths in trust and intimacy.

At a conference later that year, I saw Karen and Jessie together and they looked the picture of happiness. Karen was radiant as she introduced us, and I was witnessing a joyous lesson being learned together.

A variation of same-gender soul mates occurred recently with Todd and Nigel. When Nigel fell in love with Todd, he was devastated when Todd did not return his feelings. Todd was content to have a deep friendship with Nigel but being heterosexual, he wasn't interested in a love relationship. They have a deep friendship now, but I've noticed that Nigel's new partner looks remarkably like Todd.

Attempting to be with someone who has a past-life history with you but who doesn't want the same level of relationship with you as you would like with them can be difficult. When this occurs, you need to seek alternate ways to master your lessons or to resolve any outstanding karma with your soul mate.

This can prove to be a test of your ingenuity as in the case of Katie and Allan. When Katie applied to sing in Allan's band, they clicked immediately. Being married, Allan was hesitant to become involved with Katie, and Katie had no intention of ruining a marriage or causing pain to Allan's wife or child. As they worked together, Allan and Katie grew closer and closer, until those around them could feel the sparks of energy between them. To enjoy their soul-mates relationship without incurring karma by causing pain to Allan's wife or child meant that they had to establish strong boundaries around their behaviour. This was very hard on both of them at first, but they were mature enough to realise that if they pursued a clandestine affair, it would only lead to lies, guilt, pain and the eventual collapse of Allan's marriage. In time Katie became more at ease with their soul-mate friendship, realising that it still offered her a level of intimacy and growth with Allan.

Keeping the long-term consequences of your words and actions in mind is essential if you want to avoid causing more problems than you're solving in soul-mate relationships.

Chapter Nine

SOUL MATE
RECOGNITION

HOW CAN YOU BE CERTAIN THAT SOMEONE YOU HAVE RECENTLY MET IS ONE OF YOUR SOUL MATES? Without past-life regression, confirmation through clairvoyance or confirmation through one of the other methods listed in Chapter 2 'Finding Proof of Your Past Lives Shared', you are left to rely on your instincts.

There is a fine line between starting a good friendship or a love relationship with an instant emotional or mental connection and resuming a karmic interaction with someone from your distant past. In some cases you'll feel a sense of recognition deep within yourself upon meeting the person concerned, or you'll ease into a friendship more naturally than usual, but these are not the only signs.

Sometimes you can resume a friendship or a relationship with a soul mate and not recognise it at first. The recognition may come when you attempt to leave the relationship before you have completed the karma, and you find it difficult or impossible to do. You may find that whatever you attempt to do is thwarted, until you return to the soul-mate relationship or sort out the issue involved.

Once again, these symptoms can occur in a co-dependant love relationship, where two people have lost their sense of selves and become one in a relationship. Upon separation, each former partner can feel like half a person, as they have left (energetic) parts of themselves behind with their former partner. This is an exaggerated version of the usual loss experienced when a love relationship concludes. This energetic abandonment of parts of yourself can account for why some people feel that they miss their former partner 10 years after they have separated from them.

I've seen situations where an ordinarily independent person feels shattered after a soul-mate love relationship has concluded, and their feelings of pain and loss run deeper than for any previous relationship. They are experiencing a loss that is older than this lifetime, and their current loss is compounded by past-life grief, making the separation process much more complex than usual.

By becoming more aware of your physical body and your emotions, you can be listening when fate is at hand, introducing you to someone whom you already know spiritually, but not in their current body form.

Fate plays a hand when a stranger gives you help or much needed assistance without expecting anything in return. Sometimes this is a soul mate repaying a debt to you or helping you without being consciously aware of his past-life motives. An example of this occurred with Brenton, whose father was not much of a role model. When he was 16, Brenton's sister, Clare, married a man who became a father figure to him. Tony took an interest in Brenton and two years later they went into business together. The business lasted three years and during that time Tony helped Brenton onto his feet, both emotionally and financially. It could be argued that it was simply a friendship where one person was a role model for the other, but Brenton had three brothers and Tony felt no obligation to assist them the way he did with Brenton.

From giving Brenton gifts, to teaching him how to manage his finances, Tony went out of his way to see that Brenton had a decent start to his adult years. This act of continually giving to Brenton was out of character for Tony, and that suggested to me that this was a soul-mate friendship.

Sometimes, although you sense a past-life connection, circumstances prevent a love relationship or a friendship this lifetime. In such cases it is possible that you are honouring a commitment made to meet again, and that you'll continue to cross one another's path until you reach a life where a love relationship or a friendship is possible and appropriate.

It is the equivalent of a three-year-old appearing in the doorway to ask if it is time to go to the party yet. The child asks every five minutes until you finally say yes, as they know it's only a matter of time before you'll be dressing them and describing to them who'll be there when they arrive.

'Will there be any cake?' the child asks.

'Oh yes. Perhaps a chocolate cake and a rainbow cake. There'll be big drinks and party poppers,' you reply. The child desires cake just as you desire to have your feelings reciprocated, and you'll try repeatedly throughout many lives until the circumstances are right for you both to resume a love relationship or a deep friendship.

Sometimes you may be completely unaware when a soul mate arrives, as I was in 1983 when sharing a small terrace house in Sydney's eastern suburbs. When our fourth co-tenant left for a job interstate, we advertised for a replacement. After interviewing more than 15 people we were no closer to finding a suitable person, when Jenny arrived to look at the room. My two co-tenants liked her immediately but I felt that she was unhealthy and unhappy in her life, and I didn't want to live with her.

'Well, since we both like Jenny and you don't, if you really don't want her to live here I suggest that you pay the rent on the fourth room until we find someone suitable,' suggested

Dominic. Knowing that I couldn't afford to pay for an extra room, I accepted Jenny and we became very good friends.

Six months later we moved out together to a house of our own and had the time of our lives. We grew closer and closer until I noticed that I could start a sentence and Jenny would finish it. I'd make a humorous comment about a situation and she'd take it one step further. I'd run with the idea and she'd take it to extremes. We were a terrible twosome together, always getting into mischief and often laughing until we fell over. She took to calling me 'petal' even when she was pretending to be angry with me.

We shared two more houses together as we found one another to be easy company. Jenny died in the late 1980s, and several months after her death I took a look into our origins, to see where we had last spent time together. I found that we had been close friends (both men) in England at the turn of the century, sharing investments and cementing a friendship which was to last several lifetimes.

In the first few days after her death I was grief-stricken, and she came to me in a dream to tell me that it was all okay, and that she was fine. I was alerted during my sleep when I heard a voice say 'Hey petal, what are you worried about? I'm fine.' It was then that I realised our friendship will continue and resume again in another life.

Had I steadfastly refused to have Jenny move in with us in 1983, I'd have missed one of the greatest friendships of my life, or perhaps she'd have turned up somewhere else in an attempt to rekindle our past-life connection.

The simplest way to identify a soul mate is through your initial feeling upon meeting them. Many people describe a type of shock, or becoming overwhelmed by emotion, longing or simply a gut feeling that fate is at hand.

You may feel an instant sense of obligation for no apparent reason, or an instant positive or negative reaction to being in the company of a soul mate. You need to distinguish between your initial sense of the person through intuition and the jolt you receive upon meeting a soul mate.

Receiving the wake-up call

Sometimes we are alert to the opportunities that life offers us, and at other times we walk blindly into our destinies, realising too late that life-shaping events are occurring around us.

An example of this was Rowan, who attended a self-development course and met a soul mate without a clue what was happening. He arrived late through the rear door and found a seat in the back row of 180 people. Ten rows ahead of him a woman had felt Rowan enter the room and she turned to look at him. She studied Rowan carefully and nudged her friend, stating that she had just seen her next relationship partner. Her friend laughed and the course continued.

During the breaks over the next five days, Rowan moved around the room, meeting most of the people present. On the third day he met Alice at the biscuit table and they started talking. He still didn't notice anything unusual except that they had a good laugh and he moved on into the crowd.

On the fourth day Alice and Rowan were part of a team that had to complete several exercises together, and then he noticed her. During the next break she asked him, 'What took you so long? I thought that you said you were intuitive?' They spent the following year together.

If you have strong ideas about how your soul-mate partner will look or act, you might miss the call to a relationship that is offering you what you want, but in another guise. The important thing is not to be so fixed that you resist an opportunity for love because it does not appear in the packaging you prefer. When it comes to love, it is entirely possible that God or the universe knows better than you do what might fulfil you spiritually, mentally and emotionally.

Occasionally clients tell me of how they dreamed about their soul mate before that person arrived in their life, and that the dreams eased the way for a love relationship to commence. Don't underestimate the power of dreams to allow you to travel forward in time and to return with valuable information about your own destiny.

In 1987 I completed a guided meditation course that included moving forward into the future for the rest of my life. I saw partners and many details and events of my life (should I choose to pursue the path that was laid out before me), including the 18 books I will write. I hadn't written anything but letters and poetry at that stage.

In 1998 I experimented with hypnosis as a method for taking volunteers forward in time to glimpse the future but with no success. I decided that in the two or three years I might spend perfecting the technique, I might write two books instead. I chose to write the books but I may return to the time experiments at a later date.

Sometimes the wake-up call can be in the form of a sudden shock. A client of mine described meeting her soul mate while visiting her mother in hospital. She was running late and as she turned the corner of the corridor she came face to face with a stranger and both of them stopped dead in their tracks. She had met her husband to be and they were married 18 months later. As they stood there in the corridor, she described a strange sense of recognition sweeping through her body and later she had the unmistakable feeling of having met before.

The joy of recognising soul mates

When you recognise a soul mate it is likely that you'll feel a deep joy within, providing that your previous times spent together were rewarding. Where there has been a deep sense of loss in a past life, instead of joy at meeting again, you may experience a deep longing or feelings of pain resurfacing from within yourself.

Most times, however, the joy rising up from deep within is unable to be contained. Serena was an example of this, having recently met a soul mate.

She sat on my sofa, sighing and looking the picture of contentment until I couldn't bear it any longer. I started by teasing her.

'I hope that sighing is not about me, as you know I'm in a

relationship,' I said.

She laughed and sighed again, a look of pure joy settling on her face.

'Well...?' I asked.

'Oh, he only has to look at me and I melt inside,' she enthused.

'That bad eh?'

'And I never thought I could be interested in surfing, but I can watch him out there for hours.'

'Watch who?' I asked.

'Brandon. He has this gorgeous smile. He's shy and he gets these dimples in his cheeks when he smiles...' Her mobile phone rang and she leapt for it in case it was Brandon. It must have been, as she was beaming as she spoke.

From the moment they had met, Serena and Brandon felt instinctively at home and they looked perfect together. The joy that Serena so obviously felt was only partly due to being in love with Brandon. It also resulted from a soul recognition of someone whom she had loved before this lifetime, and someone who returned her feelings.

'I've finally found someone who seems to understand me right through to the core, and who doesn't judge me,' she said after the phone call. I continued to tease her.

'Perhaps he is judging you but he's not telling you what he thinks because as you mentioned, he's shy.' I said.

Ignoring me, she continued. 'I can't find any fault with him either. He's simply perfect.'

'And how long have you and Mr. B. known one another?' I asked coolly.

'Ten weeks now.'

'Then I'll ask you if you've found any faults with him in a year from now.'

'Oh, you're just a cynic,' she said.

Over the months that followed, there were issues to be resolved in Serena's relationship with Brandon, but they both knew within themselves that this was more than just another love relationship, and they were both prepared to work on each issue as it surfaced.

Serena hadn't found any real faults with Brandon a year later and these days she still sits out on the rocks watching him surf, only now she has company – a small would-be surfer who is eager to get into the water. Baby Brandon is a compact version of his father and I've taken to calling him B2.

There is a distinct line between the first or romantic stage of a love relationship and the joy experienced at recognising a soul mate from a past life. Soul recognition goes much deeper than romance, to the core of your being.

In one case, a friend of mine, Giselle, met her soul mate and in order to be ready for the level of love they were to experience together, she had to shed some ingrained beliefs about life and some stored grief. Within days, Giselle had been hospitalised with a bad asthma attack as her body started a process of detoxification. She found herself crying for no apparent reason and she experienced sleepless nights wrestling with her core beliefs.

For a few weeks, Giselle thought that she was going mad, until the process slowed to a halt, and she felt clear and clean and ready for the love relationship she desired with her soul mate. Throughout the process, Giselle never faltered in her desire to be with her soul mate, although it appeared that it might have a debilitating affect upon her long-term health.

The releasing of grief, resentment and old patterns of behaviour was necessary for Giselle as she prepared for her soul-mate love relationship. Instead of waiting for your relationship to appear before you go through a similar process, why not prepare yourself for the love relationship you desire by doing the necessary work on yourself now?

Preparing yourself for a soul-mate relationship can take the form of improving your physical health, resolving outstanding issues from past relationships or overcoming any barriers you may have toward intimacy. Some issues will not present themselves until a soul mate arrives, as you may share past-life issues with that person that have not presented themselves before in this lifetime.

The deep, inner joy often experienced when you encounter a soul-mate love relationship stems from a knowledge that fate is at hand, leading you down your spiritual path. Your soul-mate is simply someone who will share that path with you for some of the way.

It is unrealistic to expect that someone will share all the steps on your spiritual path with you, but between the soul-mate friendships and your soul group that shares other activities with you, you need never be alone on the path for long.

Recently a friend invited me to attend a Buddhist gathering that involved some Tibetan monks who were visiting Australia. As I arrived I felt the warm, nurturing energy of the centre engulf me. People from all walks of life were gathered together to remind themselves and one another of the importance of their spiritual foundation in life. There was an energy in the rooms and in the outside courtyard that dispelled any feelings of aloneness and seemed to dispel any inner hunger. Tiny lights sparkled in the trees, adding a sense of magic to the evening, and candles lined all the tall, garden walls, flickering in the breeze as their light was doubled, reflected in the window panes.

Spending time with those who share your spiritual perspective of life is essential to dispel any feelings of loneliness and to encourage you to traverse the path toward your own spiritual destination. This is necessary because you may find a soul mate who has shared past lives with you but who has no interest in your present spiritual beliefs or life direction. You may have certain things in common but also divergent interests. If you are able to allow one another the necessary independence to find your own friends, acquaintances and your soul groups, your love relationship has a good chance of blossoming, despite the differences.

An example of this occurred with Olivia and Charlie. Olivia was very disciplined about her spiritual development, meditating every day and ensuring that she surrounded herself with spiritually uplifting people, while Charlie was the reverse. He loved nothing more than a couple of hot pies and a pint of lager after work, and he usually watched sport on television on the nights Olivia attended her meditation group or a psychic development circle.

Despite their differences, however, they have a deep commitment to one another and to being together in a love relationship. To ensure that they are fed emotionally, mentally and spiritually, they each have their own circle of friends. In Olivia's soul group, she has people who challenge her and encourage her towards improved meditation and psychic development, whereas Charlie's group is made up of people who share his love of sports and the outdoors.

Being with your soul mate doesn't mean that you have to share everything together. Different interests allow you to have different soul groups who feed you in ways your love relationship doesn't.

The soul's joy at recognising a soul mate can sometimes be accompanied by fear, as unlikely as this sounds. The fear of being loved, and of losing the one who loved you on a deep level, can paralyse some people, preventing them from pursuing their soul mate. I have looked into the eyes of those stricken with terror at meeting a soul mate and it was a harrowing experience. It seems strange that someone might run away from the one thing everyone seems to seek in life, love. But then you hear the words of those who are running. Sandra explained it this way:

'It panics me to even think about him. I'm unable to sleep at night. The terror stalks me in my sleep and during the daylight hours.'

'What is it exactly that terrifies you about loving him or being in a love relationship with him?'

'If he didn't love me, it would be easier, believe me. You see, when he loves me in the way that I see that he does, it is very painful. It reminds me of all those times I desperately needed some love and found none. It doesn't heal me of those times. It only makes them all surface again. Believe me, there are lots of those times, so his love for me is more painful than my yearning for love and being alone. Does this make sense?'

When she described it that way, it did make sense, but I could not explain to her that one of the most powerful ways to resolve such feelings was to allow them to sweep through your body until they settle again. She was terror-stricken by something as pure as soul-mate love because it reminded her of all the emptiness from past experiences still unresolved within her.

Another example involved Edward, who sat before me quietly crying about having run away from what appeared to be a soul-mate love relationship. His big hands shook in his lap as he bit his bottom lip to control his impulse to cry.

'What were you feeling when you left?' I asked him. Taking a few minutes to compose himself, he reflected.

'She…had this way of looking at me that made me think that she was looking right through me. It was scary.'

'And did she ever tell you that she didn't like what she saw in you?'

'No. No, she didn't. But I'm sure that it was only a matter of time before she discovered something she didn't like.'

'So how long were you together in the relationship?'

'Just over 10 months.'

'And in that time she never criticised what she saw in you?'

'No, she didn't.'

'So what about the possibility that she was looking right through you, but that she liked what she saw?'

'It's possible I guess. But the feeling of panic I had was so strong I just had to get away.'

'Could it be that when you look into yourself you don't see what she sees and you don't like what you see?'

'Yes,' he sighed.

Edward's fear of being criticised and rejected prompted him to abandon what was essentially a good relationship, and this is not entirely uncommon among soul mates.

The theory is that most of us are seeking a soul-mate relationship that will exceed all other love relationships in depth, intensity and understanding, yet when such an opportunity arrives, sometimes we run away from it as fast as we can. Before you ask for, or seek out, a soul-mate love relationship, ask yourself if you are prepared for it.

If there is some inner work to be done to prepare yourself for your next soul-mate relationship, do it now. The better prepared you are emotionally, mentally and spiritually for your soul mate, the greater your chances of a successful love relationship. As the saying goes: 'Luck is where preparation meets opportunity.'

I regularly hear about how ready people are and how life refuses to deliver their soul mate to them, but some probing often reveals that although they believe they are ready, they are not. From the person who is afraid of losing his or her independence within a love relationship to someone who has not forgiven a gender for a past betrayal, there are many reasons why you may not be ready for your soul mate.

If you are not emotionally available or willing to pursue a soul mate when he or she arrives in your life, you'll still feel a deep joy at recognising them. The relationship may not develop, however, as opportunities don't usually wait for too long if they are not pursued.

Chapter Ten

SAYING 'NO' TO A SOUL-MATE OPPORTUNITY

❧

IT IS POSSIBLE TO REFUSE A SOUL-MATE OPPORTUNITY AS YOU ARE UNDER NO OBLIGATION TO PURSUE ANY SITUATION THAT IS LIKELY TO WREAK HAVOC IN YOUR CURRENT LIFE. If you have recently married and you meet a soul mate who wants a love relationship, there is likely to be some emotional fallout if you pursue such a relationship. Refusing such a relationship may be the responsible alternative, despite the possibility that you may not be able to pursue it again this lifetime.

If your soul-mate friendship is interfering with your love relationship then it may be time to set some boundaries so that you are not creating a situation in which your partner feels abandoned or ignored by you. Refusing a soul-mate friendship or relationship is usually more common when there has been an unpleasant past-life interaction between you both.

If you have been past-life enemies, or one person has betrayed the other in some way, it is likely that you'll want to avoid the opportunity to resolve the past-life karma, as it may well be a painful experience for both of you.

Saying 'no' to the lesson and to the opportunity usually means that you'll be presented with it again at some later stage, but not necessarily in this lifetime. Being aware of what you are feeling when meeting or interacting with soul mates can help you to know ahead of time what is coming your way. In 1983 I sensed that if I allowed Jenny into my life as a co-tenant it was likely to end in pain, so I resisted the opportunity, and as it turned out, I was right. It wasn't pain stemming from something she did to me, but instead the pain I experienced when she died. Even if I had known how painful it was going to be, I'd still say 'yes' if the opportunity presented itself again, because the pleasure of our friendship was infinitely greater than the pain of losing her.

Before you refuse a soul-mate opportunity, it's best to determine what your history is with the other person, and what lessons are offered to you by their appearance in your life. Determining the spiritual lesson involved can be difficult, as you need to be detached from your own life to glimpse the lessons clearly.

This is where past-life regression or a good clairvoyant reading can help you to discover the lesson with some detachment. It is too easy to decide for yourself that a soul-mate relationship is offering you a particular lesson without seeing the situation objectively.

Once you have uncovered the underlying lesson within the soul-mate relationship or friendship, you are free to accept or refuse the lesson, and to decide whether you want to have the soul mate in your life. If you decide to refuse the lesson and the opportunity, it is best to ask your spirit guides or the clairvoyant you are consulting to illuminate the underlying lessons, and what other ways are open to you to learn the lesson or to resolve the outstanding karma.

Refusal of a soul-mate opportunity is also likely if the timing is wrong. An example of this might be that you meet a soul mate who wants a love relationship while on your honeymoon.

Past-life enemies

When we think of soul mates we usually think of two people who are in love with one another and have been in love together for centuries. But what about those who bear past-life grudges for unresolved issues stemming from past-life relationships?

Past-life enemies with unresolved issues can meet again in order to address the outstanding lessons between them, and their meeting can be in the form of a friendship or love relationship. If it takes the form of a love relationship, it won't be long before the past-life issues resurface in one form or another. An example of this occurred with Carl and Rachel. At first glance it appeared to be another case of a jealous and possessive husband preventing his wife from having her own friends and her own life, but upon closer scrutiny, another pattern emerged.

Through a series of hypnosis regressions, it became obvious to Rachel that she had been in relationships with Carl previously, and that things had ended badly three times. The case that may have affected Carl most deeply was the lifetime in which Rachel (then a man) drowned in a local river while out collecting wild berries one afternoon. He was swept downstream, never to be seen again.

This unrecognised fear may have been one of the causes for Carl's unshakeable belief that one day Rachel would disappear without warning or trace. Rachel repeatedly assured Carl that she wasn't planning to go anywhere without him, but he remained unconvinced.

In one of the other lives they shared together, their relationship had ended in betrayal when Rachel (then a woman) was caught having an affair. In the present life Carl, exhibited a deep distrust of Rachel and soon cut her off from her friends and family. Arguments followed as Rachel fought to maintain her independence and to reassure Carl that her independence was not a threat to him or to their love relationship.

The unresolved past-life issues between them were colouring their present day relationship and without acknowledging these issues, they were rapidly descending into the roles of tyrant and prisoner. Although technically not enemies, Carl and Rachel had three previous attempts at an enduring love relationship which ended in pain and loss each time. Their meeting this lifetime hinted at this as Rachel was keen to pursue Carl, and Carl avoided her for the first four months after their initial meeting.

A clearer example of past-life enemies being brought together to complete particular lessons occurred with Kieran and his father. During a past-life regression it surfaced that Kieran and his father had shared a past life together where they had fought to gain the love of a particular woman. Kieran had won and they had become bitter enemies as a result.

In this lifetime Kieran's father has consistently thwarted his every attempt at pursuing his goals, leaving Kieran frustrated and depressed. When this past-life issue came to light, Kieran was able to understand how his father might have felt when Kieran had won the heart of the woman he desired. It was then necessary for Kieran to find a way to resolve the underlying issue between himself and his father so that they might move beyond their periodic battles of wills and cooperate more harmoniously as family members.

Are we obliged to pursue soul-mate relationships?

In most cases you have a choice about pursuing a love relationship, even a soul-mate relationship, but occasionally things occur too rapidly for you to realise what is happening. Sometimes, before you know it, you're deep into a love relationship with someone you met only a month before.

An example of this occurred with Max, who dreamed repeatedly as a nine-year-old boy of feeling trapped. The dream involved a red tram making its way down a hill towards the sea.

As he travelled down the hill, he felt trapped in a life he didn't want. As a nine-year-old, Max couldn't make any sense of the dream, but it came back to him one day when he was overseas as an adult. He held the rails with one hand and glanced out at the sea below as the bright red tram made its way slowly down the hill. His heart was sinking faster than the tram as he realised that this was his dream made real. He determined to get out of the town as quickly as possible, but the next morning it was a public holiday and everything was closed for a long weekend. He was now physically trapped in a town he wanted to leave.

That night, after dinner in his hotel dining room, Max walked around the town and when he came across a small bar packed with revellers, he decided to stop for a quick drink. That quick drink turned out to be a lot longer than he anticipated, as he met Claudia in the bar and they married in a local church a year later. Four years after that, Max felt trapped in the town and in his marriage. His dream as a child had turned into reality and despite his initial attempts to avoid his destiny, Max had fallen into a soul-mate love relationship.

Seven years later, Max left the town and remarried, and, looking back at that period of his life, he sees it as one that he had to experience and that his dreams of it as a child were glimpses of his life to come.

You are under no obligation to pursue a soul-mates love relationship or any other love relationship, but sometimes life overtakes you and before you can blink, you have taken steps in a direction you never intended to take.

When Clare met Lewis, she detested him at first sight. She freely admitted to me that she found him to be an obnoxious, self-centred overgrown schoolboy and she was quick to rebuff his attempts at winning her over. When Lewis first tried to speak to her, she ignored him and took out her mobile phone to make a call so that she would not have to further their conversation. During their second meeting at a conference, Lewis attempted to chat to her again and she cut him short with her most withering look and the comment 'I'm allergic to losers and as you stand there I'm breaking out in a rash. Could you stand further back please?'

Lewis was shocked by her bluntness and walked away. They met a third time, however, during another conference that included teamwork exercises for management skills. 'I hope you're good at managing losers,' Lewis said to Clare when he realised that she was the team leader for the day's exercises. She glared at him and yet as the day progressed she came to admire his team spirit. He in turn was taken by her ability to plan and to put her plans into practice directly, and without too much force.

The team exercises the following day re-ignited Lewis's desire to be with Clare, so he made a few phone calls and arranged for a friend to appear with a bunch of wilted flowers and a box of out-of-date chocolates in the form of a 'Loser-A-Gram'. Presenting the wilted flowers to Clare was an unshaven man with a hacking cough and a perpetual sniffle who picked his nose, confirming to her that there was someone more offensive than Lewis.

Afterwards she agreed to have dinner with Lewis, and he confessed that keeping up a continual supply of dead flowers was not going to be easy. They have been together for three years now and Lewis laughingly points out that it was a relationship that could only get better after the first meeting.

The receptionist in Lewis's office still saves all the wilted flowers for Lewis to take home to Clare as it has become a running joke with them. Clare jokes that their wedding will be cheap to cater for; at least, where the flowers are concerned.

When soul mates cannot be together this lifetime

Sometimes, in the pursuit of a love relationship, both partners continually find that they cannot become a couple, despite their genuine desire to be together. An example of this occurred with George and Cynthia.

George met Cynthia during sailing classes, and at the time he was married with two children and Cynthia was leaving a relationship. Deeming it unfair to leave his wife with two young children, George didn't pursue a love relationship with Cynthia.

They both felt very attracted to one another, but exercised restraint.

Seven years later George and his wife separated amicably, and George threw himself into his career as a way of coping. Another two years passed, and George and Cynthia crossed paths again when they attended an industry function. Cynthia was happily married and although they felt strongly attracted to one another still, George and Cynthia did not pursue a love relationship, due to Cynthia's commitments. Four years later George moved overseas to live and as fate would have it he moved into the town where Cynthia now lived. Cynthia was separated from her husband but George had started a new relationship one year before. Again they found that one partner was single and available while the other was already committed.

This can occur when soul mates cross paths but have no lesson to share this lifetime. The continual reconnections are to remind them that their time will come, but if they force the issue and leave their current partners for one another, the resulting pain can cause more karma than it resolves. Had George left his wife and children when he first met Cynthia, he'd have to return to resolve the karma of abandonment felt by his wife and two children. That means that three more soul mates would be waiting for him to resolve some issues and to understand the pain he'd caused them.

One of the simplest ways for us to understand the pain we have caused others is to feel the same pain ourselves. It's not the only way to learn, nor is it the easiest, but it is often the most common way for humans to learn something thoroughly.

Seeing the bigger picture, George was able to delay his desire for instant gratification and reduce the emotional fallout from his actions. In some cases those involved feel compelled to abandon their current commitment in favour of a deeper relationship, but, if the soul mates are not destined to share their paths this lifetime, any relationship between them will soon falter. This can lead to everyone involved (both directly and indirectly) being bruised by the course of events.

How do you recognise the difference between a soul-mates opportunity and the desire to escape the drudgery of your life and your commitments? It is a fine line between mastering spiritual lessons together and pursuing a sexual liaison without regard for the consequences. It might be appealing for a man in his forties to exchange his wife and family for a 23-year-old blonde and a red sports car, especially if he could write it all off as being a part of his spiritual path. It might make life easier for a woman to trade her husband for a newer model with low mileage and better prospects, but we are straying from soul mates to playmates.

That's not to say that it's unlikely for men and women to meet their soul mates in later years and leave their long-term partners. As humanity progresses spiritually, it is possible that long-term relationships will be shorter as we realise our lessons earlier and move on toward other opportunities for spiritual development. Alternatively, we may expect less of one another and this might help relationships to last longer as we meet some of our needs, such as friendship and spiritual fulfilment, outside our love relationship.

Accepting that you cannot be with a particular soul mate this lifetime is easier if you keep in mind the bigger picture. Realising that you have opportunities to be with other soul mates this lifetime can ease the suffering experienced when you know who you want to be with but are unable to fulfil your desires.

If the timing is wrong, there is nothing to be gained from forcing the issue regarding a soul-mates love relationship. Perhaps you can accept a friendship instead, or, if the pain you are experiencing is too great to be near your soul mate, you may need to sever all contact with them this time around.

Only rarely can you hold onto that which is not rightly yours this time, and, if you are meant to be together at some point, an opportunity to be together will present itself. Perhaps not in this lifetime, but that is something you may have to surrender to, in order to pursue your own spiritual path in life.

An unusual example of poor timing occurred with Dawn and Ted, who met and fell in love in the 1930s when Dawn was married to Peter. Dawn summoned all of her strength to remain with Peter, and Ted moved away and later married. They didn't see each other any more, although they thought of each other often in the years that followed.

After Peter died, Dawn found it hard to manage in the house on her own, at 71 years of age. Her daughter found her a suitable nursing home and she sold the house and moved in. One afternoon as she sat on the verandah watching a sunset, she heard a laugh that she recognised. It was Ted, who was visiting a friend.

Dawn sat staring at Ted and his friend for a few minutes, her heart pounding with anticipation and excitement. After a few minutes she couldn't bear it any longer and she slowly made her way down the wooden boards to where Ted sat.

'Excuse me for interrupting you, but is your name Ted?' she asked gingerly.

'Dawn?' he asked, his eyes widening. He stood up and they held one another for a minute before standing back to look at one another.

Now Ted has more reason than ever to visit the nursing home and he explained to me that his passion for Dawn had not dimmed through the years they were apart.

Chapter Eleven

VIVE LA DIFFERENCE

SOUL-MATE LOVE RELATIONSHIPS DRAW PEOPLE FROM DIFFERENT COUNTRIES, CULTURES AND AGE GROUPS TOGETHER AND THIS SOMETIMES COMPLICATES THESE RELATIONSHIPS. Different cultural backgrounds can cause initial conflict within a relationship but if both partners are willing to make allowances, most issues can be resolved.

An affinity for a country where you have spent past lives can draw you to the people of that country, as you may find their culture and way of life attractive. A soul-mate relationship with a partner from a culture you have lived among in previous lives can strengthen the relationship, all other things being equal.

Being born in the same generation as your soul mate is not always possible, so you may find yourself attracted to someone who is 10 or 20 years older or younger than yourself. Although a marked age difference may present practical issues to be resolved, such as when each partner wants to start a family or when partners pursue particular career opportunities, the depth of a soul-mate connection may be enough to overcome these concerns. This means that next time you see a 50-year-old woman in a love relationship with a 32-year-old man it is possible that they are soul mates who have been born a generation apart. It has long been acceptable for an older man to pursue a younger woman, and now the same rights are being afforded women. Where eyebrows may still be raised when a 52-year-old woman introduces her 33-year-old partner, the reaction is less noticeable than even 10 years ago. Hopefully in 10 years from now, there will be no reaction at all. It is necessary to keep in mind that outsiders rarely see what relationship partners find attractive in one another.

Religious differences can be a more complicated issue between relationship partners but with negotiation and tolerance they, too, can be resolved or allowances made. Dietary and lifestyle differences are becoming more potent issues in long-term relationships as the following example illustrates.

Sharon was a strict vegetarian whereas Bob loved his eggs and bacon for breakfast, and then roast lamb on Sundays for lunch. At first Sharon agreed to make these for Bob, but in time she grew resentful and it became an issue between them. Bob jokingly told Sharon to think of it as bacon-flavoured tofu but the joke soon wore thin. To resolve this, Sharon ceased cooking meat for Bob and they agreed to eat out for lunch on Sundays, where Sharon was able to order a decent vegetarian meal while Bob ordered as much meat as he could eat.

Chapter Twelve

FIRST LOVE ~ THE EMOTIONAL FOUNDATION

A S WE MATURE THROUGH ADOLESCENCE, WE OFTEN FORM OUR BELIEFS ABOUT LOVE RELATIONSHIPS THROUGH OBSERVATION OF OTHERS AND THROUGH FIRST-HAND EXPERIENCE. These years can leave us with anchors that make us initially attracted to people with certain physical attributes.

One night I asked some friends what physical attributes they found attractive and the responses surprised me. Marianne said that she found a gap between the front teeth appealing. Donna said that she found hairy men attractive. The more body hair the better, as far as she was concerned. Charles said that he loved red hair. Masses of bright red curls could stop him in his tracks, regardless of the person beneath the hair. Zoe said that she preferred men with one long thick eyebrow, which met across the nose, while Jasmine found short men attractive.

When I asked them why they found these attributes attractive, they couldn't tell me. When I asked where they first encountered someone with the attributes they now find attractive, the answers varied. Some said that their mothers or fathers had these attributes, while others mentioned a first boyfriend or girlfriend. In almost every case, with careful questioning, the person traced the desire for a particular attribute back to someone in their past.

This brings us to anchors. When we experience intense emotions such as powerful love, fear, anger or grief from loss, we may unconsciously form associations with other things that surround us at the same time. When falling in love, for example, you might associate a person with an aftershave or a perfume and each time you smell that scent, thoughts of the person spring to mind.

An example of an emotional anchor occurred with Rick as a primary school boy. Rick was often in trouble with teachers during breaks as he played in the schoolyard, and was told to go to the head teacher's office to await punishment. The head teacher's office was behind the staff lunchroom so Rick waited outside the lunchroom throughout many a long lunchtime. As he waited nervously, he usually smelled tea brewing, as the staff drank tea during the break. Rick soon associated the smell of tea with a sinking feeling in his stomach, as he stood apprehensively awaiting his fate at the hands of the head teacher.

To this day the smell of tea in a teapot makes Rick feel nauseous and drinking unscented or unflavoured tea makes him feel ill. This is simply the result of him forming an association between his feelings as a child and the smell of hot tea brewing. These days when Rick wants a cup of tea, he drinks Earl Grey tea or herbal teas, as these have different scents and he has no negative associations with them.

If Rick can make an association between the scent of tea and impending trouble due to his heightened state of being as he stood in the corridor as a child, you may form similar associations through your initial love relationship experiences. If these associations or anchors go unchecked, you may find yourself attracted to people who look or act a particular way, but who have nothing in common with you. During our teenage years, many of us experienced our emotions more intensely than at any time since early childhood, and, as a consequence, anchors or associations may have been being formed continuously.

The advertising industry knows this, and that's why 1970s and 1980s songs are used to accompany advertisements for luxury cars today. Those creating the advertisement realise that many of their potential buyers who were teenagers in the 1970s and 1980s are now in the income bracket to afford such cars. The soundtrack to the advertisement is hopefully a positive anchor for the target audience and the advertising agency hopes that with repeated exposure, a new association is formed with the luxury car.

Without questioning your associations or anchors, you risk walking through life being half-asleep. Being a prisoner to your anchors can limit your choices, so it's important that you observe your anchors regularly and desensitise yourself to the strongly negative anchors.

An example of desensitisation to negative anchors occurred with Kieran, the four-year-old boy next door. Kieran was a passenger in a car accident that required a trip to hospital and several stitches in his bottom lip. From that day forward every time his parents wanted to drive somewhere they had to struggle with Kieran, who fought vigorously to avoid being enclosed in the family car.

I decided to help Kieran to establish a new anchor with cars, after his strongly negative association with them resulting from the accident. One afternoon he was bored in the back garden and I decided to wash my car. I asked him to help me, explaining that we weren't going to drive it anywhere, but just wash it where it stood. Soon Kieran was splashing about with the bucket of soapy water and he had a great time hosing it down afterward. As it was drying I decided to vacuum the interior and Kieran once again proved eager to help. With all four doors open, together we cleaned the interior.

After completing this, I decided to clean the inside glass of the windows. Kieran sat in the back talking to me as I wiped the glass down with a linen cloth. I then closed the doors one by one as I cleaned their windows, and Kieran didn't seem to mind.

After completing our task, we locked the car and went inside for ice-cream. Kieran had spent almost an hour inside the car, part of that time with the doors closed, and he didn't panic, because he knew that we weren't going to drive anywhere. He sat there talking to me and asking me about the ice-cream we were planning to eat after the job was done. He was forming a new association with cars, which with repeated practice, eventually helped to dissipate the anchor resulting from the car accident.

When you leave a disastrous relationship, chances are that you'll have several positive and negative anchors that were formed during your relationship. After the grieving period, it is important that you examine these anchors, to decide consciously whether you want them to continue in the future. They'll affect your future whether you look at them or ignore them, so you may as well know what they are, in case they restrict you in the pursuit of love relationships.

The following exercise is designed to help you to recognise what anchors or associations you may have from previous love relationships. You'll need a pen and a pad for this exercise.

Emotional anchors exercise

1. List five things that remind you of your first love. For example, an aftershave or perfume, particular clothing or a car.
2. List any particular or unusual physical attributes that you find attractive in a partner.
3. When did you form these associations?
4. Who was the first person in your life to possess these physical attributes?
5. What things act as a negative reminder of a difficult past love relationship?
6. Is it important for you to redress these anchors? If the anchor was for an aftershave that is no longer produced, you may

choose to ignore it, as it is unlikely that you'll encounter it again. If, however, the anchor is an association between physical attributes and negative behaviour patterns, you might consider redressing it.

7. Do any of these anchors inhibit you in your pursuit of a love relationship?

8. In what way (if any) are you inhibited in the pursuit of a love relationship by these anchors?

The first step towards removing any power that anchors have over you is to acknowledge what the anchor is and discover how it was formed. Anchors and associations are formed naturally, and even positive anchors may limit you in perceiving life and opportunities clearly. If you have a powerful positive association with a particular aftershave, it may lead you into a relationship with someone who wears it before you have considered whether that person is suitable for you as a partner.

Negative associations are often more powerful but these can be challenged through new experiences. An example of negative anchors being challenged occurred with Harry. Harry is a friend who views all lawyers negatively. He believes that they are all liars and cheats, and I asked him the following question one day: 'Who will you phone to represent you if you are falsely accused of a crime and arrested? How will you feel about lawyers then?' He pondered this for a few minutes and nodded. He realised that a lawyer's expertise might be useful and honestly used one day. All he'll need is one strong, positive interaction with a lawyer and he'll be singing their praises.

Reviewing your negative associations with particular people from your past is one step towards remaining open to all that life offers you, but this must be done within reasonable boundaries. I'm not suggesting that you find a positive association with someone who has treated you sadistically or who has made your life a misery, but that you challenge the tendency to dislike anyone who looks like the person who has mistreated you.

I recall a conversation between two strangers at a party that illustrates this. In anger, one man turned to the other and stated loudly: 'I hate you and everyone who looks like you.' He was stating that to him, physical likeness meant inner resemblance.

Positive anchors can also cause difficulties. I mentioned earlier in this chapter that Donna found hairy men attractive. She also stated that kindness was an attribute she sought in a partner. It is safe to say that not all hairy men are kind-hearted. Donna's positive association with hairy men may lead her to assume that the next hairy man is also kind-hearted. In her case she traced her love of hairy men back to her father. She recalled the hot afternoons spent swimming in the sea with him, laughing and watching his hair floating on the surface of the water. Later she remembered the smell of his hair drying in the sun as they lay on the sand and talked. During precious moments shared with her father, Donna subconsciously formed an association with his hairy body and what a kind man looked like.

When asked what their ideal partner might be, many people described a composite of past positive partners' traits. They then added to this their unfulfilled hopes for those people they did not have a relationship with but whom they desired. This formula often leaves out many possibilities that may fulfil them.

They sometimes ignore opportunities that didn't fit their preconceptions because they have no experience with them, preferring instead to stick with what they have tried rather than to explore the new. For this reason, I try to have my son look at life from as many perspectives as possible. The more he experiences as a child, the more things he is familiar with, should he choose to narrow his focus of opportunities only to those things that he knows.

Food is a classic example of this. He told me one day that he didn't like eating fish, and I was happy to accept this. A week later we were eating out at a cafè and I ordered a smoked salmon bagel. He was curious.

'What's that?'

'It's a chewy bread, shaped like a doughnut, with smoked

salmon, cracked pepper and lemon juice and it tastes fabulous.'

'I'll have one too.'

'Okay, but if you don't finish it; it's mine.'

Without mentioning that smoked salmon was fish, I managed to have him try the bagel and he loved it. When I pointed out to him afterwards that it was fish, he asked me why it tasted different to the other fish he had tried. I explained that there are many varieties of fish and that this salmon was smoked instead of being grilled or fried. I pointed out that even though he didn't like fish, he might discover two or three types that he loved. 'I don't like fish but I do like smoked salmon,' he stated a week later. One of his negative anchors had been challenged.

Your negative anchors may be as subtle as a gentle breeze or as powerful as a tornado. The effect of these anchors depends on you.

Another friend, Lauren, described her positive association that led to a life of relationships with Mediterranean men. Lauren's first job as a 17-year-old was working in a fruit shop. The owner was an older Italian man who took great care of her and doted on her like she was his own daughter. She developed an infatuation with another worker, also Mediterranean, who was closer to her own age. After 18 months working there, Lauren left to enter the hotel industry, never having fulfilled her desire to have a relationship with her co-worker.

Almost every love relationship since then has been with a Mediterranean man, although Lauren is not Mediterranean herself, nor of Mediterranean parents. I teasingly suggested that she never dare to visit the Mediterranean, as she is likely to be married within 20 minutes of leaving her hotel room. Her positive association with the older man and her attraction for the younger man combined to form a powerful positive anchor regarding Mediterranean men.

Attraction to types

Most of us have particular types of people to whom we are attracted. We may be attracted to physical features, physical height, accent, colour of skin or physical build. Every so often it is important to re-examine the type you are attracted to, in order to see if your initial attraction is leading you towards fulfilment or frustration.

Years ago I was reading for a Pacific Islander who was a large, well-rounded, enthusiastic woman. I glimpsed (clairvoyantly) an image of her digging holes for fence posts on a property on the island where she lived, doing all the manual work herself. In the background I saw a man who was staring at her admiringly. He seemed to be very attracted to her size and her capability. I asked her if the Islander men preferred large capable women and she laughed, telling me that the men often rested while the women worked. In her community, she was the desired type.

I have a friend who has a fondness for large front teeth, and I describe him as a mammal enamoured with enamel. During a visit to Europe he sent me a postcard from Amsterdam that read: 'Everyone here has big teeth. I must have died and gone to heaven. I'm never coming home so tell everyone to forget that they ever saw me. I've got to go. Someone is smiling at me. (Sigh).'

Often the characteristics to which you are attracted are the result of initial love relationships or initial attractions to people around you in your teenage years.

Another friend of mine, Courtney, finds men who are sensitive, artistic and lost, very attractive indeed. I have often teased her by wearing a beret and waving a street directory around, claiming to be lost, artistic and perhaps too sensitive ever to be found.

The type of people you initially find attractive may not suit you at all, so it is time to examine what appeals to you and how you formed those initial anchors. Continue the emotional anchors exercise with the following questions.

9. What physical features or characteristics in a person do you find attractive or irresistible?
10. Who was the first person you found attractive who had these physical features or characteristics?

> 11. Did you find what you sought in relationship or friendship with that person?
> 12. What do you need to do/say/hear/experience in order to resolve any outstanding desires you have for that person?
> 13. Will speaking to that person or writing them a letter (which you may choose to burn rather than post) resolve any feelings you have within for that person?

If you need to write a letter to a past friend or partner, do so now, before continuing.

When I ask clients how they can resolve issues with people they have not seen in 15 years, they usually tell me that it is impossible. I jokingly tell them that high school reunions are designed for those who seek one last chance to explore an unrequited love and this is sometimes true.

If you seriously wanted to trace the whereabouts of someone from your past, no matter how distant, it is possible. Whether it is necessary is another thing, but if you feel that you cannot lay someone in your heart to rest without speaking to them then you owe it to yourself to do so.

Unresolved past loves (especially unrequited ones) make for heavy emotional baggage when you want to enter a new love relationship. If your heart is filled with feelings for someone in the past, there is no room for someone new, unless they resemble your past love. There is no point in drawing someone new into your life if you are going to starve them of love and affection because you have not overcome someone from your past.

If you return to a past love, you take a big risk. There are three basic possibilities:
1. You will both realise that it is a love relationship worth pursuing and you'll pursue it.
2. You'll have all of your romantic illusions stripped away as you see the person with new eyes. Realising that this is not to be, you can freely move on to a new relationship.

3. You will want to pursue a love relationship with the person, but they will be unavailable or unwilling to do so. This will allow you to then ask yourself what you believe that they can give you in a love relationship, and to ask yourself what you need to do to accept that they will not give you what you desire.

Most reasonable adults think nothing of carefully planning their career moves, taking time to ask themselves what they want from career and what they will give to a career in return. Many of these reasonable adults do not apply the same logic to securing the right love relationship for themselves. Why?

I believe the difference between Western attitudes to love relationships and to careers is that much of our relationship information is absorbed as children, when we are less equipped to filter out what we don't like or to question why things are so. Our gathering of career information usually starts in high school, when we are old enough to question what we want and what we are prepared to put into achieving our goals. Not all of our ideas about career are formed in the teenage years, as I found one afternoon when I asked my then five-year-old son what he wanted to be when he grew up.

'I don't know,' he replied.

'Perhaps you'll want to write books like me,' I ventured.

He looked at me haughtily and said, 'I don't think so.'

It was then that I realised that my son wanted a 'real job' and that he believed that I was whiling away my life on some folly of an enterprise that was going to lead to no good. At five years of age he had strong ideas about what is worth doing as a career. Who knows, perhaps he'll be a sobering influence upon me and I'll give up writing for a career in banking?

14. Casting your mind forward, how do you perceive your soul-mate love relationship in three or four years, after the initial passion has waned?

15. Do you want to have children with your next soul mate partner?

16. If your soul-mate relationship partner arrives tomorrow afternoon, will you be ready for them and for the relationship that follows?

17. List all the qualities that you seek in a soul mate. Ensure that you list the obvious qualities also. If you are a woman seeking a man, then state that you want a man who is single, available and heterosexual. If you are a woman seeking a woman, state that you want her to be also seeking a woman, and that she is comfortable with her sexual identity. There's no point in meeting the person of your dreams only to find that you are the wrong gender for them.

18. Now list below what qualities you can offer a soul mate. For example,. loyalty, independence etc.

There is no point asking for a sports-minded partner when the closest you ever come to sports is a dash through the supermarket once a week. If you receive a sporty person, he or she will be off competing with others while you freeze on the sidelines or wait at home wondering if you are still in a relationship. (If they are very sports-minded, they'll probably only beat you at tennis, sailing, hang-gliding, surfing and you can forget about arm wrestling.)

Think carefully about whether you want a complementary partner or one who is similar to you. Both offer opportunities and both require compromises. If you are lethargic and you find a similar partner, you'll never get out of bed on Sunday mornings. After reading the papers you'll probably have another coffee and then fall asleep for a few hours before watching a film while propped up on pillows and eating ice-cream.

If you are lethargic and you find a complementary partner, they'll be energetic and enthusiastic. This might mean that they drag you out of bed early on Sunday morning to play a round of tennis and then on to an afternoon of sailing. This may well improve your blood circulation and make you glad that you did get up early. Alternatively, your energetic partner might leap out of bed on Sunday, leaving you to sleep in, and another day passes without one another's company.

If you are energetic and so too is your partner, then adventures await you both. Parachuting or bungy-jumping from bridges at night is all the more enjoyable when you have someone special to share it with, but the downside comes when you have exhausted all of the adrenalin-triggering possibilities. Alternatively, competitive people often compete with those close to them, and such competition inhibits intimacy.

Consider your most significant past (or present) partner and tick the list of qualities below that he or she has shown, and tick the qualities that you possess in a different coloured pen.

independent	practical
competitive	even-tempered
loyal	hot-tempered
sensitive	distant
compassionate	cynical
critical	messy
honest	neat
broad-minded	organised
narrow-minded	well-presented
ambitious	unkempt
focused	health-conscious
indecisive	a forward planner
emotionally strong	sentimental
easily overwhelmed	disorganised
serious	cold-hearted
responsible	musical
entertaining	a good communicator
financially irresponsible	a poor communicator
avaricious	vengeful
generous	forgiving
romantic	controlling

open to directives	strict
a morning person	enjoys foreign cultures
an evening person	a leader
creative	opinionated
self-absorbed	forthright
enjoys social gatherings	idealistic
prefers own company	enjoys family life
likes reading	prefers independence
likes films	fashion-conscious
diet-conscious	fashion indifferent
enjoys alcohol	politically aware
charismatic	politically indifferent
shy	religious
a good talker	atheist
a good listener	spiritual
sensual	likes parents
passionate	dislikes parents
spiritually minded	likes children
meditates	dislikes children
scientific	prefers city living
logical	prefers country living
adaptable	loves the sea
in good health	sporty
a homebody	open to self-development
loves the outdoors	resistant to self-development
enjoys travel	blames other for failures
adventure travel	takes responsibility for failures
needs comfort when travelling	enjoys career
enjoys a variety of foods	dislikes career
prefers favourite foods	cannot pursue chosen career
plays a musical instrument	wants children
optimistic	has children
pessimistic	doesn't want children
forgiving	cannot have children

Although the previous list may seem unnecessary, it only takes one or two differences and a love relationship becomes a tall ship bound for rocks in a storm. If one partner wants children while the other already has children and doesn't want any more, then problems may result. If one partner loves socialising and the other prefers solitude, it requires that both partners allow for one another's differences. If the social partner insists that the other accompanies them to social functions, only one person will be happy. If the quiet partner insists that the social one stay at home with them every weekend, then again only one partner will be happy in the long term.

It isn't necessary that both partners are identical in tastes and lifestyle choices; only that they can happily make allowances for the other partner to do what they need to do. Naturally this open-minded approach can be taken to extremes at times, by partners who want to pursue behaviour that is damaging to the relationship.

I recall one client telling me that her husband had sat her down one afternoon to explain that he had a higher sex drive than her, and that she should allow him to pursue other women to meet his sexual requirements. He wanted her to sanction these affairs and she had consulted me to ask if she was being unreasonable in saying 'no' to his demands. To put it all back into perspective for her, I asked her two questions:

'What year is this? Are we back in the 1970s?' I then explained to her that mature men are aware that entering into an exclusive love relationship allows for a deeper intimacy and that only boys think that more is always better.

Lasting relationships are about negotiation rather than control. The above list is to determine what you have in common and which areas require that you become adaptable or make allowances. Before you assume that you want a certain type of partner, ask yourself if that type has brought you happiness or misery in the past.

An example of past love relationship patterns being unfruitful occurred with Diego who was a sensitive photographer. In the past he had been attracted to wild, adventurous women who rode horses and motorbikes, and who liked a bit of rough and tumble. It occurred to him one day that he was too sensitive for all that, and that life was likely to be more peaceful if he found someone who wasn't staring off into the wilderness in search of their next adventure. These days Diego still notices the adventurous types, but he is aware that adventure is usually accompanied by cuts and bruises. As he bruises easily, it's better for him to find someone who enjoys a more comfortable existence.

In *Palmistry Revealed* (Simon & Schuster Australia, 1996), I outlined the personality types according to the hand and the sort of person each type gets along well with. Some people like to be admired by their partners while others feel safe with someone they can admire as a leader and achiever. Other types prefer to work hard in a business with their partner toward a common goal, while some prefer to be swept off their feet by romance. While some just want a partner to look after their basic needs, others need an intense physical, emotional and spiritual passion where they are free to examine the darkest corners of the soul of their partners.

Before you can truly decide what type of love relationship suits you, you need to examine your needs carefully. Do you enjoy heady romance? Are you embarrassed by displays of emotion? Are you jealous? Are you possessive? Do you seek to release the pain and accept the grief you feel or do you take revenge to new heights?

There is no point pretending that you want an unconditional love, because if you desire it then it is only right that you offer it in return, and this rarely happens in love relationships. We seek a love relationship to meet our needs, and that means there are conditions to the relationship. Chances are that if enough of your conditions are not being met, you won't pursue the relationship for long.

If enough of your needs are being met in a love relationship or you feel that they can be met by a particular person, you'll usually pursue it through thick and thin. So identifying your needs before you start a relationship makes sense. It's the same with a career. You probably wouldn't work at a job that paid $4 per week less than your bus fares to and from work because at the end of the week you'd have given your time and energy but be worse off than before you started.

Chances are you feel the same way about love relationships. If you continually give time, effort and energy, and at the end of each week you are worse off than before you started, then it's probably only a matter of time before you leave, or collapse with exhaustion.

Preparing yourself for a soul-mate love relationship may take a week, six months or several years. The time you spend in preparation may well justify the wait, especially if your needs are met and you happily meet your partner's needs.

In the process of writing this book I circulated the previous questionnaire to friends and their friends, and their responses surprised me. It was not that most people I spoke to didn't believe in soul mates, but rather that they didn't believe in love relationships that worked.

'If you can find a relationship that lasts 10 years these days, you'll be lucky,' said one.

'And if you do find a long-term relationship, look deeply and you'll find a mortgage and kids. That's why they're staying together,' said another.

'Four months is about my limit,' said another person, unaware of how cynical she was sounding.

'My soul mate is my dog,' said another. 'He's the only one who's stood by me through thick and thin.'

'If I want romance, I rent a video – something sentimental. The desire for romance usually passes within a few days.'

I wondered aloud why I was bothering to write a book about soul mates when people seemed so jaded about love and the possibility of a long-term relationship working. When some of those people heard this they were quick to reassure me that they would read such a book, only that it would be unlikely to change their beliefs about love relationships.

I started to re-examine my approach. I wasn't promising a love relationship that lasted forever. I wasn't asking them to suspend disbelief or to become overly romantic. I believed it was a level-headed approach and that with effort, readers might resolve past issues that consumed present-day emotional and mental energy, and prepare themselves for the love they needed to further themselves spiritually. Realising that their past actions and desires probably affected the present, I started asking about first loves, and the emotional anchors they set up for life. (See page 67.)

Preparing for your soul mate

I often hear from people who are desperate to be in a love relationship and who are still single. These are not people who are content to be single, even for a year or so. They are hungry for a love relationship and yet their desires seem to elude them.

'Where are all the available men?' I overheard a woman ask during a lunch break on a recent course.

'They're married,' replied one woman.

'Or gay,' added another.

'Or both,' another stated flatly, and they laughed.

Conversation turned to how they planned to pursue their goal of finding a suitable partner and to their credit, they had many of the available options covered. They regularly dined with friends, especially in mixed company. They joined clubs, travelled, searched the Internet, attended sporting events and one woman confessed to having membership of three gyms, in the hope of meeting some men.

As I listened to their conversation it occurred to me that with the level of exposure they had, and the fact that they were intelligent, approachable and well-presented, there must be some hidden reason why they weren't finding the men they desired. I pondered this for some days before returning to my theory that all things that can be done with physical effort, can also be done with energy.

Everything has a distinct energy to it, including riding a bike through a leafy park on a lazy Sunday morning to a first date at a restaurant with a near stranger. I began to closely re-examine the energy of the women who had been discussing men during the recent course and I wondered if on some deeper, subconscious level, they were not ready for a new love relationship. Then I turned to my counselling clients, and to clients consulting me for clairvoyant readings.

During one reading, a woman named Claudia asked what the future held for love relationships, and I told her that I could not see a new partner for her within the next two years (the prediction span of the reading). Claudia seemed upset by this, and declared that she was well and truly ready for a new relationship.

I scanned her past for unresolved issues which might prevent her from entering a new love relationship and sure enough, there were several issues. The first of these was that Claudia had grown up believing that she would marry one man for life, and when she married and then divorced, it was in conflict with her core beliefs about life. Deep down, Claudia believed that any relationship following her marriage was not to be a lasting relationship, as she had already finished her one chance at fulfilment. It wasn't logical and when I pointed it out to her, she agreed with me that it didn't make sense. It was, however, a core belief, and as such, it was affecting Claudia's love life and was set to continue to do so until she changed the belief.

The second underlying issue was that it had been 19 years since Claudia had been a single woman, and she felt out of her depth with dating. Claudia's desire to meet a life partner was strong, but her fears and her core beliefs were preventing that life partner from reaching her. It's easy to say 'get a grip' or 'change your core beliefs', but more often than not, core beliefs are hidden and you see only the results of these beliefs. I suspected that with Claudia's core belief about one relationship for life, she might update her dating skills and make herself available for a love relationship without success. Core beliefs about life are very powerful and unless they are serving you well, they need to be updated or replaced.

The following exercise is designed to help you to recognise those forces in your life that may have shaped your core beliefs about love relationships and your right to be loved by another person. This last sentence may appear extreme, but I can state clearly that as a counsellor, I have seen more than a few people who fundamentally believe that they don't deserve to be loved. With that core belief, a deep loving relationship is impossible, as such people end up sabotaging anyone who tries to love them. Don't assume that you know what your relationship core beliefs are, as completing this exercise may surprise you. You can skip the exercise if you are enjoying a well-balanced soul-mate love relationship at present.

Core beliefs exercise

As many of our core beliefs about life are formed before seven years of age, we will start there.

1. Were your parents still happily married when you reached your eighth birthday?
2. If they had separated, what age were you when they separated?
3. Did you live with either separated parent before 10 years of age?
4. Did you live with a stepfather or stepmother as a child?
5. What was your relationship with your father like as a child?
6. What was your relationship with your mother like as a child?
7. What was your parent's relationship like?
8. What (if any) issue was a constant source of tension between your parents?
9. How did your parents resolve issues between themselves?
10. How do you resolve issues between yourself and your partner when in a love relationship?
11. Name any other role models you had in the first 20 years of your life and list how they inspired you.
12. If you could resume any past love relationship, which relationship would you choose?

13. What did that love relationship offer you?
14. What do you miss most about being in a love relationship with that person?
15. Name the person or people with whom you desired to pursue a love relationship that did not eventuate?
16. What did you hope to receive from this person or people?
17. What (if anything) did you hope to receive from your relationship with your mother that did not eventuate?
18. What (if anything) did you hope to receive from your relationship with your father that did not eventuate?
19. What do you hope to receive from a soul-mate love relationship?
20. What do you hope to offer or contribute to a soul-mate love relationship?
21. What issues are unresolved within you from your most recent love relationship?
22. What issues are unresolved within you from your first love relationship?
23. Carefully reflect upon your current lifestyle. Do you have time for an intimate love relationship or would a casual relationship better suit you?
24. List all the things a partner has asked you to give up in past relationships. (For example, sport, friendships, family, career, hobbies or travel plans.)
25. Are you prepared to give up these things again to be in a love relationship?
26. If not, how can you ensure that you can maintain your interests and goals while in a soul-mates relationship?
27. What problems or issues have your past relationships had in common?
28. How will you ensure that your next relationship does not replicate your previous relationships with common unresolved issues?

Chapter Thirteen

IS HAPPINESS PART OF THE PLAN?

WHEN I ASKED OTHERS IF HAPPINESS WAS PART OF THEIR PLAN WHEN CONTEMPLATING LOVE RELATIONSHIPS, THEY ALMOST ALWAYS REPLIED THAT IT WAS. Yet when I observed the large number of unhappy love relationships, I was led to believe that there might be other unseen forces at work when we select our love relationship partners.

From a conscious viewpoint, those questioned told me that they sought love, understanding, humour, compassion, a companion, a mental challenge or simply good sex, but I observed that more often than not, in some of these things they were disappointed. When I probed, there did seem to be several forces at work.

The first of these was unresolved issues from past love relationships, surfacing in a new relationship and wreaking havoc. Gustav explained to me that his relationship with Heidi didn't stand a chance, as he was still emotionally shattered after being betrayed by his previous partner, Carol, who had an affair with his best friend. Trust issues soon surfaced in the new relationship and Heidi felt that Gustav was becoming increasingly possessive of her. The resulting arguments soured any good feeling they had for one another and they parted company.

Unresolved negative patterns of behaviour stemming from childhood are also strong forces that shape our love relationships. As a child, you observe the adults who serve as models for how love relationships will be for you in later years. If the adults in your household are cold and unkind to one another, tolerating each other for the sake of the children, then it is increasingly likely that you'll have a similar love relationship when you're an adult, unless you challenge and change those behaviour patterns.

Taking the unresolved issues even further, it's possible that unresolved issues from past lives with particular partners or even from past lives generally will be an unconscious force, driving you toward a particular partner or type of partner. And what of the biological forces at work? What about our unconscious desire to have healthier, better-looking or more intelligent offspring than ourselves and the possibility that we pair with people whom we feel will increase our chances of having such offspring?

Being unconscious, these desires can be powerful forces in shaping our choice of partner, the type of partnerships we choose, and whether we have children with those partners. With the advent of contraception, we have more choice in when we have children and whether we have a family at all, but this does not necessarily affect our subconscious desire to pair with someone who will help us to produce children with the desired qualities.

When you take into account the unseen forces at work in your selection or pursuit of a partner, it is worthwhile asking whether happiness is a part of the plan. What is the likelihood of your being happy in love with someone you have unconsciously chosen to pair with for their genetic qualities? With these unconscious biological forces at work, it is increasingly likely that if they go unchallenged you may end up with varying levels of unhappiness in your relationship but with good-looking and healthy children.

So much for nature's plan for us to reproduce the species. What about our plans for ourselves? More and more of us are choosing not to reproduce and some of us are past the age of reproducing and yet we are searching for a fulfilling love relationship. Those of us for whom reproduction is not an issue may be still unconsciously governed by our biological make-up unless we set about consciously deciding what our primary needs are within a love relationship.

In nature's plan for reproduction of the species, there may be no place for happiness but as we evolve as a society and the threats to the survival of the species are reduced, we can introduce happiness as a priority in the pursuit of a life partner.

Our ancestors have long pursued love relationships but the expectation of long-term happiness in a love relationship is a relatively new thing. In the past we married to reproduce, to preserve the family fortune, to have children to provide for us in our old age, and only sometimes because we were in love. But the modern expectation that we can resolve to leave one another if we feel emotionally or spiritually stifled by a partner is a concept that has developed only in the last 80 years. In the past (for women particularly), it was an ill-considered plan to leave a husband, as women had fewer opportunities to provide financially for themselves and their children if they left their husbands. These days, in many cases, women have more real choices when it comes to leaving an unhappy marriage or relationship, as they have more financial opportunities and in some countries men are bound by law to take some financial responsibility for their offspring.

Having real choices and alternatives if you find yourself in a dead-end relationship can sometimes allow you to 'give it one last shot' before giving up all hope of being together.

The desire to reproduce the species has to be one of the most primary urges after self-preservation, or the human race would have disappeared into history long ago. So now we have several powerful forces working at once as we attempt to find a long-term soul-mate love relationship. We have the primary need to reproduce, the need to be loved and understood by another person, and an unremembered history shared with several people from past incarnations. If these needs are in harmony with one another, it is likely that a love relationship will form easily and flow gracefully toward deeper commitment between those involved.

If however, the partners have conflicting needs, a troubled relationship often results. If one partner's need to reproduce drives them toward a partner who differs in physical or emotional make-up from their soul-mate partner, the soul-mate relationship has a diminished chance of success. If one partner does not feel loved or understood by the other, then the soul-mate relationship is less likely to continue. Finally, if the past lives shared between the soul mates were lives of great pain and suffering caused by one partner, the other partner may feel unconsciously wary of entering into a love relationship.

A pleasant completion of karma is occurring with two friends of mine, Caroline and Eric. They are as much in love today as they were when they met 53 years ago. They share a mutual respect for one another and it is a joy to see them together.

Caroline described meeting Eric and knowing instantly that this was the man she was to marry. They first met in a hospital where Caroline was visiting an uncle. Eric didn't notice Caroline at first, as he was convalescing after being a prisoner of war in Europe for several years. Despite the fact that Eric was thin, frail and confined to bed, Caroline knew that with love and support he could become the writer he dreamed of being.

After a week it was apparent to everyone that Caroline was visiting the hospital to spend time with Eric. Her uncle didn't mind, telling her that blossoming love was what every hospital ward needed; to motivate the patients to heal and to return to life and all it promised them. They married a year later and it was another 15 years before Eric published his first book. Now in their seventies, Eric is still writing and selling much of his work while Caroline works from home as a natural therapist.

The question you must ask yourself is: 'Is happiness a part of my plan for love relationships?' And if not, then why not?

Are all spiritual lessons painful?

When others tell you about how much they learned from a situation, they are often telling you about how much pain they endured in an incident in their lives. Sometimes they have learned from their experiences, and sometimes they are desperately searching for meaning in the pain of an experience.

We cannot seem to believe that painful situations can be random or without meaning to anyone but those involved, and so we search for patterns, thoughts or deeds that may have contributed to our pain or loss, or a greater sense of the universal plan. Sometimes we are satisfied that we have found a pattern or a spiritual lesson behind the events, and sometimes we search in vain throughout our lives for a reason.

Many of the questions we ask ourselves are perhaps too big to be understood, and yet we ask anyway. When I saw a mother with a seven-year-old daughter who was suffering from leukaemia, I could not answer her when she asked me why. It's such a simple question but still it's too big to answer with any certainty.

When an older woman asked me why her husband had to live through the holocaust and spend time in a prison camp, I could not answer her. I had trouble even grasping the enormity of his suffering. She said that he lived his whole life with guilt for surviving when most of his family had died. She wept as she pondered that the only difference between his dying in the camp or dying many years later was that it had taken him a lot longer to physically die than the others. She said that he was one of the walking dead for every day after the war until they buried him.

There is no way to confidently state that there were no spiritual lessons for those who have died or suffered in wars, but there is no way to state with certainty that there were spiritual lessons either. It is unlikely that many people live to become adults without pain and suffering and yet the question arises; is suffering the only way to master spiritual lessons?

Can we learn through joy or through play? Children learn a great deal through playing, both alone and with others. It is possible that spiritual lessons can be learned through joy or through play but if these lessons are continuously refused, they often approach us again in the form of pain. There is nothing that quite focuses the attention like pain; especially physical pain. If you drop a heavy object on your toes, all other concerns fade from your conscious mind immediately.

When someone you love dies, the loss can consume your conscious mind and your awareness. In attempting to avoid the pain of the loss, you might focus your thoughts and attentions on some practical concerns such as your career but doing this doesn't prevent the pain from reaching you. It either reaches you in dreams at night or it awaits an opportunity to resurface.

When you commence a soul-mate love relationship, there is a real risk that you will experience pain as well as joy, and if the relationship concludes you may be left with painful and rewarding memories of your time spent together, learning lessons and loving one another. At first the painful experiences may be foremost in your mind, as concluding a love relationship or even loving someone involves risk and sometimes pain. But with distance, the joyful experiences may surface, to be remembered alongside those things that caused you pain.

Perhaps it is human nature to recall painful episodes more clearly and readily than joyous incidents in the past?

A friend of mine attempts to avoid experiencing too much joy in the hope that this will lessen the pain he is likely to experience. We argue about this often, beause I believe that in old age he will have to live with the regret that he did not immerse himself in those glorious moments when he was loved or understood by another person, or those times when he felt that he truly made a difference to someone.

The polar opposites of pain and joy bear closer scrutiny when you consider how pain seeks you out whereas joy needs to be discovered or pursued. It has been argued that pain gives us the emotional depth to appreciate joy, but at what point does pain become so unbearable that no amount of subsequent joy will make any difference to your existence?

It is as though slight pain carves out a hollow in a log where joy can later reside. Too much pain, however, carves through the log, breaking it into useless pieces where no joy can reside. The joy that follows such pain spills over the broken pieces of wood, sinking into the rich, dark earth beneath. All that remains is the evidence of unbearable pain.

How do we measure emotional and spiritual pain? Is there any reliable comparison between those who have great emotional and spiritual strength and those who don't because they were crushed by pain too young, too soon into this incarnation?

During a recent clairvoyant reading, I was describing to my client a former friend of hers, who missed her. The client had recently cut ties with many of her friends and acquaintances as she felt that they were stifling her spiritual growth. I searched for a way to describe the woman I saw clairvoyantly and the only words that came were these: 'She is very self-centred. She wants others to understand the pain she has seen but in fact she has seen very little pain in her life. She thinks that she's the only person ever to have suffered when in fact she has barely suffered yet at all.'

My client smiled and nodded. 'That's exactly what I came to decide a few months ago. She was sapping my emotional strength and I was tired of being used by her. I had my own problems to sort out.' Later it occurred to me that comparison of pain is virtually impossible. Through association with past incidents, a small current event may have great significance and cause great pain whereas a major loss or upheaval may be accepted easily.

Insisting that all incidents occur due to karmic forces is perhaps an oversimplification of life. If you take this logic to its extreme, then it is possible to justify your ill intent with the rationale 'If I am meant to kill my neighbours in a hail of bullets, then it must be their karma.' Some might argue that shooting your neighbour was creating karma that will have to be addressed later, but who can safely assert that you are not fulfilling your neighbour's karma?

A more simple view of pain and love relationships is that perhaps we experience pain until we get it right. Perhaps when we truly understand ourselves, our needs and our purpose, we can step around those things that might cause us pain in favour of those opportunities for growth through joy.

Opportunities for joy exist around us constantly and we need to attune ourselves to searching for those opportunities. The exercise below is designed to awaken you to those things which give you joy. If you cannot find enough things to give you joy then you need to try five new things or experiences every week until you have a list longer than your arm.

Learning through joy

Why do we need to examine joy in a book about soul mates? Because much of our Western training is about seeking a life partner who will make us feel better about ourselves and our lives. This is not only erroneous logic but can be a recipe for depression and resentment. If you are miserable, a new love relationship can only temporarily relieve you of your misery. Sooner or later (usually sooner), you discover that you are miserable once again and that your newfound partner has failed you in your bid to be happy.

If you are already filled with joy, then a love relationship becomes a bonus and not a necessity. You are likely to ask less of your partner because you are already happy, and less strain is placed upon your newfound love. Nothing kills love and spontaneity as quickly as demands and expectations, so fulfilling many of your own needs allows your love relationship to maintain some of its mystery and allure.

Maintaining a balance between our needs to survive comfortably and to find joy in life can be difficult at times, and this chapter is a reminder of the need for joy.

Sounds often lift our spirits, whether it is the sound of the spoken voice, music or the sounds of nature. The following examples illustrate some of the ways in which sound brings joy.

Many years ago I started a relationship with a girl whose primary hobby was bell-ringing in the churches and cathedrals of England. Through her I gradually began to discover the joy that groups of people derived from standing in a tower ringing bells in sequence together to form tunes. It was a deafening but exhilarating experience.

When my son was small he loved to hear me tell him funny stories, and he soon became my most demanding critic. The conversation often went this way:

'Dad; tell me a story.'

'Okay. Are you comfortable?' (Shuffle, shuffle.)

'Yes.'

'Once upon a time there was an enormous forest.'

'No, Dad. A funny story.'

'Okay. Three lemons huddled together at the end of a thin sinewy branch of the lemon tree, looking for a way to jump across to the orange tree to play with the oranges who'd been teasing them earlier in the morning.'

'No. Funnier than that!'

'Give me a minute. It gets funnier as it goes.'

'Okay then,' he'd say, ready to cut me off if it didn't get funnier soon.

Ten minutes later I'd have him falling off the sofa from laughing so hard, and I'd end up being glared at by his mother for bringing on an asthma attack. He didn't care as the joy of the story was worth the loss of breath and the bruise from landing on the floor with a thud.

Most children like to have fun and they know it. They actively seek it out and yet many of us lose the sense of the importance of joy in keeping us alive later on in life as adults. I find it puzzling that the top Hollywood awards are rarely given out for comedies, and more often for dramas. When you consider how easy it is to make someone cry and how hard it can be to make them laugh, why do we give more weight to dramatic books and films than humorous ones?

Sources of joy exercise

1. From where you are standing or sitting reading this book, glance up and cast your eyes around you. Notice how many things in the room or directly around you offer you joy. List them on a separate piece of paper.
2. List the things from Question 1 from which you have also derived joy in the past seven days.
3. What has been your favourite period of your life so far?
4. What things brought you joy then?
5. List the things that once brought you joy but which you have given up or not pursued recently?
6. What are your favourites tastes?
7. What sounds, songs or pieces of music bring you joy?
8. When you were younger, what did you promise yourself that you'd do in the future to bring you joy?
9. In the past five days, how often have you seen an opportunity for a joyous experience and postponed the opportunity? List each opportunity for joy.
10. If you felt free to do whatever you truly wanted to do right now, what would you choose to do?
11. Why aren't you doing what you have listed in Question 10?

Sometimes in waiting for the glorious opportunity for long-lasting joy, we miss the smaller chances to gather happiness to ourselves. The answers to the previous questions are a guide to those things that bring you joy. What you choose to do with this information is entirely up to you.

If it's not asking too much ~ a guide to asking to learn through love

Spiritual lessons need not be painful. Many lessons that become painful can often be learned more easily earlier on in life. It is our continual ignorance of the underlying lessons in life which make them repetitive and painful.

Many people seem to have the concept that when they meet their soul mate they'll never have to make an effort again. They believe that paired soul mates share everything from similar tastes in music to favourite foods, films and countries to visit. When I hear such things I ask myself, 'Where is the learning in that?' It sounds idyllic but often the creation of heaven on earth is a recipe for disaster. A simple observation will confirm that great creativity usually requires conflict or tension to assist in its production. Without any frustration, humans often lack impetus to move forward toward new goals, spiritual or otherwise.

Some people have the greatest capacity for creating misery out of the best ingredients, and a love relationship is no exception for them. After commencing a soul-mate love relationship, they find fault with their partner and ignore the potential of the relationship and its spiritual lessons. An example of this is a friend, Carl. After a few years spent longing for a deep and lasting love relationship, Carl met Andrea and they fell in love. From the outset it was apparent that they were well suited to one another, and this in itself turned out to be Carl's greatest fear confirmed. If Andrea was well suited to him, Carl had no reason to look for love and to yearn to have his needs met, as Andrea was right beside him. Thinking that he might soon be crowded by Andrea wanting to move in and live with him, Carl tested the waters. He suggested that Andrea move house and she refused. 'I'm quite happy where I am,' she replied, much to Carl's relief. Faced with the possibility of being loved and understood, Carl panicked and sought reasons to leave the relationship. It appeared that he was more interested in yearning for love than actually receiving it.

Time after time, we sat and discussed how it might be for him to have a love relationship with someone who loved and understood him without judging him, and each time his face lit up expectantly, like a man in search of the Holy Grail. Being in a relationship with Andrea, who by Carl's own admission, loved and understood him without judgement, Carl's needs were not met as he expected they would be. Every week he seemed to find another reason not to allow himself to surrender to the love that Andrea offered him, until I suggested that perhaps Andrea was not the woman for him and that it might be wise to leave her and to continue his search for love. Carl immediately grew more attached to Andrea with the thought of losing her looming in his mind, and a new pattern emerged. It appeared that Carl was able to seek love and was prepared to work hard to hold onto a relationship that he thought might be slipping away from him, but he appeared to be unprepared to actually receive love when it was offered.

The getting and the holding onto parts Carl knew well, but the receiving part of love he had failed to grasp. He sat before me complaining about his need for love so I asked him a few pertinent questions.

'Let's see if I have this clear,' I said to him. 'You are in love with Andrea, and she's in love with you. You want to be together and you are together. You wanted someone who loves you but who doesn't judge you and Andrea fills these requirements. You wanted someone who doesn't prevent you from enjoying the company of your friends and Andrea is happy for you to spend time with your friends. You share a love of the same foods and films and yet you have enough differing interests to make life interesting for both of you. Where's the problem?'

'Er, now that you put it that way, I don't know.'

'I think the problem arises when you stop longing for someone to share life with and start accepting that new person into your life. To receive the love they have for you, and allow them to offer you small kindnesses. That's what love becomes eventually; a series of simple kindnesses.'

Embracing the lessons offered in a soul-mates relationship can be one of the joyous avenues to learning. Realising that the person you love will only share some of the steps on the path with you can help to prevent you taking their love for granted.

Chapter Fourteen

YEARNING
FOR LOVE

❧

THOSE MOMENTS OF WISTFULNESS WHEN WE PONDER OPPORTUNITIES PASSED, RELATIONSHIPS CONCLUDED AND FRIENDSHIPS ABANDONED CAN FEED US MOMENTARILY, BUT THEY CAN ALSO TAKE US AWAY FROM THE PRESENT, WHERE OUR CURRENT OPPORTUNITIES LIE.

Over dinner recently, I asked some friends what things filled them with yearning, and the responses were not at all surprising. One person said that she yearned to be loved and understood by someone special, while another said that she sought an unconditional love. One person ventured that she desired to be loved like a child and protected from the onslaught of life with the knowledge that they were a team, meeting challenges together. She conceded that this was probably a replacement for her childhood relationship with her deceased mother, but yearning is not necessarily a carefully planned thing.

Another fellow diner yearned to have a partner who understood the different parts of him, from the achievement-oriented man to the dreamer. I suggested that this was a lot to ask of a love relationship partner and he nodded. 'Tell me about it. I've been searching and yearning for almost 30 years now.'

So why do we expect one person to fulfil all of our love needs? Is it possible to have friends who fulfil some of our needs and a partner who fulfils the rest?

Suppressing an inner yearning is not the answer, as such deep hunger often relates to real needs that seek fulfilment. Our deepest yearnings can be the motivation for great books, films, or other works of art, and the creation of these things can sometimes fulfil our desires. Throughout dinner, I continually distilled the yearnings of those around the table until it appeared that we had arrived at one common goal — to be loved and understood by another person.

If a soul-mate love relationship is one where we are loved and understood by another person then this relationship offers a solid foundation for our emotional development. Such a relationship is likely to further our development spiritually in the most positive way imaginable, and yet few of us seem to be able to maintain such a relationship for long.

When we yearn for perfect love, we rarely imagine the efforts we will have to make to maintain such a relationship and the risks we will have to take to allow such intimacy. When our yearning becomes reality we may be consumed by fear of intimacy, of loss, or of being revealed to another person; and in turn we may shrink from the thing for which we yearned. We may instead sabotage our chance for a fulfilling love relationship.

Yearning is possibly a temporary way out of a situation, out of a difficult period in your life, or out of an uninspiring life. With minimal effort, you can slip away from your physical or emotional circumstances and return in your heart and mind to a past love, a place or a time, to re-live it as it was or as you wanted it to be.

Yearning for an achievement, real or imagined, for acknowledgement, for spiritual realisation or for inner peace is something familiar to many of us, along with the yearning some of us experience for respect, for resolution of an issue or simply to belong. The exercise below is designed to help you to discover what things, places, and feelings of achievement you yearn for, and from this understanding, you may set out to fulfil a yearning before you meet your next soul mate.

For what do you yearn?

1. When you are faced with continuing frustration and few solutions, do you slip away into yearning for some other time or place?
2. Is there someone (or several people) from your past that you yearn to be with again?
3. If you could spend an afternoon with that person, what would you say to them?
4. How can you release these needs from within yourself, in order to move on with your life and your current opportunities?
5. Do you yearn for a particular achievement?
6. Can you achieve this goal independently of a relationship partner?
7. Would being with a relationship partner make this goal more rewarding to achieve and to share?
8. When you have achieved this goal, what will you have then?
9. How much of your current life is spent yearning for someone or something that you do not currently have in your life?
10. Is yearning a reminder to you of what you want on a deeper level or is it a chance to escape current circumstances?

When given the time to explore their deeper desires, most people yearn for something. This yearning may change daily, according to the circumstances and demands that life places upon them. During days when the phone won't stop ringing and I have editorial deadlines, I yearn for a small cottage by the sea, where I can sit by the fire and write uninterrupted. I envisage stepping out into the day to collect more logs for the fire and to sip hot tea as I stare out across the water at a wooded headland far off in the distance.

Yearning to be loved and understood is perhaps one of the strongest reasons for people seeking soul mates. Finding someone who loves you for your soul or spirit can feed you on the deepest level imaginable, if you allow it.

Chapter Fifteen

WHEN SOUL
MATES PART

AFTER THE RELATIONSHIP CONCLUDES, YOU HAVE CHOICES AS TO HOW YOU RELATE TO ONE ANOTHER. If young children are involved, there may need to be an ongoing relationship despite ill feeling between former partners, and if lessons are not mastered together, there may be a recognition of more work to be done together at some later date.

The ideal, of course, is to recognise that we are all travellers on the spiritual path together, and that any chance to help one another is an opportunity to strengthen ourselves also. This can be easily forgotten in the bitter recriminations that sometimes follow a relationship break-up.

When I asked clients how their soul-mate relationships concluded, the responses varied.

'Bitterness to the power of four,' replied Amelia, shaking her head.

'We just looked at one another one day and agreed that it was over,' sighed Louise. 'Then we made lists of the things we wanted from the house and sold the house and moved away from each other.'

'He told me that he'd met his soul mate and I told him that any willing 25-year-old bimbo looks like your soul mate when you're in your forties,' stated Karen through clenched teeth.

'I looked into her eyes one day and noticed that I wasn't in there any more,' sighed Don. 'It was then that I realised we were soon to part.'

Because soul-mate relationships are more intense than other love relationships, the ending of such relationships is often more emotional. In some cases, the partners feel overwhelmed with grief and loss for someone they cannot stand to be in the same room with, and this can be due to the hopes they started out with and the realities they are left with as the relationship concludes. If they haven't completed their karma or mastered their lessons together, they'll be back to finish these at some later date.

Keeping the bigger picture in mind helps you to understand that although you may not have learned all that you hoped to learn from a particular relationship, life needs you somewhere else to learn other lessons and to be open to other opportunities. Naturally it would be simpler if life told us exactly when our final opportunity approached us, but life is rarely that transparent, even to clairvoyants.

Sometimes soon after the lesson is learned and partners in a soul-mates relationship separate, they look at one another and wonder what they ever found attractive in each other. When the lesson has been mastered the attraction can sometimes fade rapidly, and this may be life's way of encouraging the partners to progress toward their new opportunities and the lessons contained therein.

An example of this occurred with Heidi, who happily ignored men for love relationships with women. Things were different when she met Erik, whom she found attractive, much to her surprise. Erik and Heidi had a three-year relationship, after which Heidi returned to women and never thought of having another relationship with a man. Perhaps Erik was the exception for Heidi as they had a lesson to learn together, but having learned that lesson, they were free to pursue new directions again.

'At first I saw it as a brief indiscretion,' stated Heidi. 'But then I realised that I was feeling very content with Erik. And afterwards, of course, I never looked at another man, especially since I met Hannah.'

How many steps do we share on the path together?

Once you've found your soul mate, it may be important to find out how many steps you share on the path together this lifetime. Some of our most intense lessons are short ones, covering only several months or a few years. Although you are soul mates and you may cross one another's path again in the future, the lessons you share may only take a short time.

One close friend and I shared many lessons and then he entered a place where I could no longer reach him emotionally. After the death of his parents, my friend became unreachable emotionally for me, and 12 years after we had been close, we can no longer communicate on a deep level. At first I thought he was suffering from reactive depression resulting from the loss of his parents, but after 10 years had elapsed I realised that our time of closeness together had passed, and his path was taking him in another direction from my own.

There is often a sense of loss when those who have been close to us disappear from our lives, but you can prepare yourself for this eventuality by determining beforehand just how many months or years you have to share on the path together.

If you don't have strong nerves then skip this section, as knowing approximately when your friend or partner will leave your life can be too much of a burden for some of us to carry around with us. I've made close friendships with soul mates who had only months to live and it was obvious that our time together was limited. This had the effect of sharpening our senses and increasing our honesty when dealing with one another, as we knew that anything left unsaid might one day be unsayable until our next incarnation together.

It occurred to me one day that this is how all my friendships and relationships might become, but it is almost impossible to live that way when human nature encourages us to take those close to us for granted. When your close friend or partner has only months to live, you may allow yourself a naked honesty and a vulnerability that you'd never dream of replicating in a relationship that might last another 10 years.

Knowing when your new friendship or love relationship will conclude may impair your ability to allow intimacy, as you may be preparing to limit your feelings of loss at its demise, instead of enjoying the moment given to you to share. An example of this occurred with me in 1990.

My then wife Amanda returned to England for a holiday and I suggested that she visit a clairvoyant I had worked with in 1988. The clairvoyant didn't know that we had married and had never met Amanda, but two minutes into the reading she was asking if Amanda knew me, as she had a clear image of me in her mind. She then went on to state that our relationship would last five years, before moving onto other questions and issues. Having that information, whether right or wrong, can influence many of your decisions during the course of a friendship or love relationship. It casts a sharper shadow over your life when things are not as good as they might be in a relationship and it may even limit the depth of your commitment to a relationship, knowing that it will be over soon. As it turned out, we separated five years later, as predicted.

I asked a friend and spiritual teacher about this prediction when I was studying with her in England in 1991, and she put it more tactfully. 'Your spiritual lessons together will last five years, and after that time you can choose to remain together or to go your separate ways. It's really up to you.'

As a palmist, it is tempting for me to examine the hands of my new relationship partners, but I realise that I'm not keen to know when we will separate, so these days I avoid looking at their hands.

With practice, one of the most effective ways to access information about your soul mates is through asking your spirit guides in meditation or through dreams. Asking your spirit guides requires repeated practice to enable you to reach deep levels of meditation where you are not imagining the outcome, nor are you distracted by your daily concerns or your hopes and fears.

Simple questions to ask your guides or your higher self in meditation include the following:

1. Is this person my soul mate?
2. What are our primary lessons together?
3. What can I offer this person?
4. What does this person have to offer me?
5. What unresolved issues do we carry between us from past lives together?
6. What is the best approach to this friendship/relationship?
7. How long do we have together this time?

To access the same information through dreams, you need to ask your subconscious mind to provide you with the necessary information about your soul mate; one question at a time. Making requests of your subconscious mind takes some time and practice, but, as you sleep anyway, spending a few minutes planning what you want isn't much effort for the results.

Before falling asleep tell yourself the following:

'Tonight I will have a dream, which I will recall easily in the morning and all day tomorrow. This dream will deal with the following issue. (Select one issue from the seven points listed above.) I will dream a clear answer to my question/issue and awaken refreshed and revitalised tomorrow with the answer foremost in my mind.'

You may need to practise this procedure for several days or even weeks, but sooner or later your subconscious mind will understand what is required of it and you'll have your answers. Don't ask more than one question at a time, as you may become confused upon awakening. Keep it simple and only move on to a new question when you have dreamed the answers to your current question.

If you consider that in some place and time all that you are about to do is already history, all you really have to do is access that place and time and you'll know all the answers. This can be done with practice, through meditation.

Being soul mates is no guarantee that the path you tread together will last for the rest of your lives. Keeping in mind the fact that you have spent time together in previous lives, it is possible that you'll spend some more time together in lives after this one, and that you may have only several years or months together this time around.

Ascertaining how much time you have together this lifetime requires great courage and it is not for the faint of heart. It is natural to expect to be together forever, and knowing that you have only several years ahead of you can be very unnerving.

It's easy to ask a clairvoyant or to ask your spirit guides how many years you will share with your soul mate, but remember that you cannot forget the answer once it has reached your ears. On those difficult days when issues arise between you and your soul mate, you might recall what you know about the number of years or months together and become disheartened by the whole relationship process.

It is unlikely that you'll be sharing the rest of your life with your soul mate as you may have several soul-mate relationship opportunities to come. Instead of becoming less interested in a love relationship that doesn't last forever, perhaps you can become determined to make the very most of the relationship while you have it.

Knowing that you won't be together forever can ensure that you don't take one another for granted. It is always sad to see a relationship partner who is being ignored, emotionally abandoned or taken for granted. Year after year of being taken for granted is enough to kill off any love you may feel for someone, and once they have been extinguished, the flames of love can rarely be rekindled.

More important than knowing how many steps you share on the path together is knowing the issues or lessons contained within the love relationship. Understanding the issues allows you to tackle them with your eyes open or to prepare for them so as to resolve them quickly. Knowing the lessons involved in your relationship also allows you to master them, and then to decide whether you want to continue the relationship after its purpose has been realised. You have the free will to choose to spend months or years with a partner after you have learned what you came together to learn.

For some people, the concept of 'no major lessons still to master' offers a promise of a peaceful time ahead whereas for others, new relationship opportunities beckon. Remaining aware of the big picture (the many lifetimes and many soul mates) can help when you are experiencing grief or loss at the end of a soul-mates relationship.

More often than not, the desire to have a soul-mates love relationship can obscure the awareness of your spiritual path and the lessons offered by such a relationship. Finding your soul group (in the form of those who share your spiritual beliefs about life) helps you to remain fulfilled during and between soul mate relationships.

To determine how long you are likely to be together in a soul-mate love relationship, you can consult a clairvoyant who specialises in past lives or who can clearly see the underlying spiritual lessons contained in your relationship. Alternately you can ask your spirit guides in meditation, as they can often outline the lessons and give you a guide as to the length of time you have together.

If you were to discover that you have six years together, this does not necessarily mean that you'll have learned your lessons in that time. Perhaps you'll have to be together again in another lifetime to complete your journey.

Knowing the lessons involved doesn't mean that your relationship has to be hard work, as love offers one of the best ways to learn. Many people associate learning with struggle, difficulties and hard to reach goals, but ask a child what learning is like and they'll probably tell you that it's play – it's all play.

Knowing the lessons you share with your soul mates is more

important than knowing how many steps you share on the path together. No-one can share the path with you in its entirety, so you have to become familiar with saying hello and goodbye to those you love.

Two people together can make it a wider, more comfortable path to tread or they can ignore the path in their squabbling and struggling to control one another. If you bear in mind that ultimately it is your path and that you have to tread each and every step to the end, you'll welcome your soul mates as teachers and friends, as you make your way to the ultimate destination.

Western civilisation seems to fuel the myth that there is someone out there who will share your whole life with you, and your entire path from beginning to end, but this is a very limiting view to hold. Can you imagine how much learning you might miss whilst treading through the weary patterns of a lifelong relationship?

The risk of building a house beside your spiritual path and ignoring the path altogether might increase if you were to become too comfortable in one long relationship. To ascertain how you are growing and developing, complete the exercise below.

Viewing your progression exercise

1. Think back to your first love relationship. (If you are still in your first love relationship, this exercise is not for you.) Do you miss that person?
2. Do you think that you could resume that love relationship as it was, at your present age?
3. Do you think that you could resume your second love relationship as it was, at your present age?
4. How have you changed during the years since your first love relationship?

The sad truth is that you can rarely return to the friends and lovers of your past and expect that things will be as they once were. It is likely that both they and you will have changed.

On my first author's tour, I returned to the city where I grew up and I telephoned some old school friends. In each case, a 10-minute conversation confirmed that I had grown in a different direction to each of them.

Although we still had some things in common, we had taken our own spiritual and physical paths and they had led us away from one another. This can also occur with soul mates. Sometimes they pair your steps on the path through a part of your life and then their own path diverges from yours for the rest of your life.

When the lessons are learned

Although the spiritual lessons contained within soul-mate love relationships may have a greater impact upon us in our lives than other love relationships, when these lessons are completed we have choices. These choices include whether we want to continue the relationship with our soul mate or pursue other lessons, perhaps with other soul mates. The intensity of a love relationship may fade after the spiritual lessons are mastered and you may feel less inclined to be with your partner.

In other cases when the lessons are learned you may feel content to be together, as the obstacles in your path (the lessons) have been solved or negotiated. An example of the intensity of a love relationship remaining after the primary spiritual lesson was mastered occurred with Dean and Kayley.

When Dean first met Kayley they fell in love immediately but their attempts to be together were frustrated by Kayley's responsibilities. Kayley's younger sister, Joanne, had been born with a physical disability and it fell to Kayley to help her sister on a daily basis. After several months in the relationship with Dean, Kayley organised a roster for the remaining family to help with Joanne so that she might spend more time with him.

Then Kayley's mother fell ill and Kayley was once again needed on a daily basis. Soon after this, Kayley's boss asked her to work longer hours as he set about expanding the business into other countries. By year's end Kayley was working 65 hours a week in the business and then helping her mother on weekends. Kayley's responsibilities included ensuring that her mother's house was clean and that she had enough prepared food for the week.

It was a testing time for her relationship with Dean, especially when Dean was transferred to the company head office in another part of Ireland. They desperately wanted to be together but life seemed to keep them apart. A distance relationship ensued for another 18 months before they agreed that something serious had to occur before they could be together. They decided to leave Ireland and move to Australia to live, leaving behind their families and all those who demanded their time and energy on a weekly basis.

After organising a new roster for the family to look after Joanne and Kayley's mother, Kayley and Dean sold their few possessions and moved away. They were careful not to fall into the same trap in their new homeland and their relationship blossomed. Looking back on their early life together, Kayley decided that the lesson was to overcome the obstacles and maintain a commitment to one another in order to fulfill the promise of their relationship. Once they had done this, the lesson was mastered, and they decided that they were happy to continue together.

Having built up a longstanding, committed love relationship, Kayley and Dean decided that a lack of pressing spiritual lessons did not mean that they had no future together. Each soul-mates love relationship has its own possibilities and requires its own set of decisions as there may be more than one major spiritual lesson underlying the relationship.

More often than not, a soul-mate love relationship involves several lessons together, and these combined lessons can lengthen the time spent together as partners. In the end it is the quality of the time shared, and not the length of it, which matters most.

In another case, two soul mates completed their shared lesson and parted soon afterward, going on to have other fulfilling love relationships. Tom and Danielle both left same-gender love relationships to try a heterosexual relationship with one another. It was tough going at first and many adjustments had to be made, but after they overcame their initial trust issues and 'found their feet', the relationship blossomed. They learned for the first time how to negotiate their paths in an equal love relationship and after they had mastered the lesson, they parted, two years later. According to Danielle, they are still good friends and she credits Tom with having taught her how to accept nurturing. Tom, in turn, reveals that he learned how to be assertive from being in a love relationship with Danielle.

At the close of a soul-mates love relationship, it is sometimes tempting to believe that you'll never love with the same depth and passion again. This is so for those who energetically leave parts of themselves behind with each partner (see *A Secret Door to the Universe* p. 170 'Retrieval of Your Senses', Simon & Schuster Australia, 1999) but most of us live on to love again.

When you consider the possibilities illustrated in Chapter 4 and the section 'The Boat', you'll recognise that with each lesson mastered, you are more available to receive love and to offer love in return. If you continue to grow and develop spiritually, there is no end to the levels of intimacy and trust that you may experience in love relationships. Although your initial innocence may be lost, it is hopefully replaced with understanding and a mature compassion for the trials and lessons of your partners and friends.

Recently I met a woman who had spent 24 years with her soul mate, and she described loving him as much in the last year as in the first. He had died five years previously and she had been walking around in a daze ever since. She seemed unable to find a suitable place for herself in the world without him, and hoped to die soon in order to be with him. I had the difficult task of telling her that although their love relationship had concluded in this lifetime, she still had other lessons to learn, and that she had many years ahead of her in which to master these lessons.

As she sat before me sobbing, she described how her whole family had been set against her marrying this man as he was 15 years older than her. She went ahead and married him and did not regret it for a single day.

I asked her what she thought the spiritual lesson was in that love relationship, and she paused before answering.

'It was love. Simply loving and being loved I guess.'

'And do you feel that to love again in that way this lifetime might dishonour the relationship you had together?'

'I don't want to love again like that. I don't think it's possible anyway.'

'Why isn't it possible?'

'I barely know another person who's had a relationship like that anyway, let alone two.'

'But you've had one relationship like that.'

'Yes. Yes, I have.'

'And if you could find one soul mate, what's to stop you from finding two?'

'Yes, but at my age...'

'There you go with age. You're starting to sound like your family now.'

She laughed and nodded. I continued to point out the obvious.

'Your lesson here on earth is to take longer than his, and that is not to detract from your relationship in any way. What you had with him is in your heart and in his soul to be taken with him wherever he goes next. Although that was a major part of your life, your life is not over yet. If you're still here, chances are you still have lessons to learn, and to master these lessons you have to embrace life again.'

In the West, life tends to revolve around one opportunity, one chance, one love.

'This is the big one' is the statement that says it all. This is your one big chance at love, happiness, wealth or the life you've always dreamed about, and after this one chance, you are doomed to live in the shadows of your actions and decisions.

We are continually given opportunities for love, wealth,

happiness and the life we've always dreamed about, but sometimes we fail to see these opportunities. How often do you see two or three suitable jobs arrive at once, or two suitable partners appear within a week of one another after years of searching? Opportunities often arrive like buses, two or three at a time. That is not to suggest that all opportunities carry equal weight or offer equal spiritual growth, but that we have more than the one chance when it comes to soul mates or any other thing in life.

Two years ago I read for Jane, who was happily married, and I told her that within 18 months a man may appear to offer her a love relationship unlike anything she'd previously experienced. She promptly told me that she was happy with her husband and I assured her that if and when the new man arrived, she was free to refuse him and remain with her husband. 'It's nice to have a choice' is the way I usually put it. It's a bit like a menu really. If you arrived at a cafè and they offered soup as their entire menu, you might feel disappointed even if the soup was fantastic, simply because you were denied a choice. I recently read for Jane again and she enthusiastically described her new man, boldly stating that this was a love relationship unlike anything she'd ever experienced.

'What happened between your husband and yourself?' I asked.

'Don't get me wrong. I still love Theo but when Damian arrived I was knocked off my feet. I knew deep within me that I had to pursue this as a relationship or I'd kick myself for the rest of my life.'

'And what became of Theo?'

'We decided to separate and we're selling the house next month. We were in a rut and I couldn't see it. When you told me about the new man I was scared. I didn't want anything that might upset the comfortable balance Theo and I had created in our lives. You know, the dogs, the cafè on Sunday mornings and dinner with friends every Saturday night. It was stable but it was also boring me to bits. I woke up the day I met Damian.'

'I guess you exercised your free will when Damian arrived.'

'I exercised every part of me,' she laughed.

Just as we have free will about our life direction when a soul mate arrives, so, too, do we have free will when a soul mate leaves our lives. After a soul-mate relationship concludes we are free to pursue other love relationships or to remain alone, reflecting upon the recent relationship.

Although for many of us finding our soul mate and enjoying a life-long relationship is the ideal, this is not always the reality. If your soul-mate love relationship concludes, you may need to be open to further soul-mate opportunities. If you believe that you'll only have one soul-mate opportunity this lifetime, you may overlook other opportunities or diminish their potential, and chances for happiness and fulfilment may be ignored or squandered.

Consider what might happen if you believe in only one soul-mate relationship opportunity and the first soul mate you met only wanted to be your friend, or was the same gender as yourself and didn't want a relationship with you. What might happen if your first soul-mate experience was to meet someone with whom you shared a past life who was honouring an agreement to meet again but who had nothing to teach you or to learn from you in this lifetime?

With this limiting belief, it's no wonder some people become depressed and despairing after a soul-mate relationship has concluded. In some cases, in order to prolong the soul-mate relationship, couples refuse to master the lessons involved, but the likelihood of the relationship becoming stale and empty grows steadily if partners refuse to learn or to progress in life.

Sometimes the lessons are only apparent after you have separated from one another, or the lesson is about how you separate from one another and how fair you are in dividing material things after the relationship has concluded. If one partner has been unfair in the division of wealth in a previous life together, the lesson may repeat itself in your present relationship, especially after the relationship has concluded. In some cases the real lessons only arrive at the point of separation and involve the distribution of wealth and possessions. How former partners do this is the subject of another book entirely.

Agreeing to meet again

Sometimes, after a life spent with a soul mate that has been fulfilling and emotionally rewarding, we agree to meet again. This is often done through a simple longing to be together again, rather than as a verbal agreement. It's human nature to want to repeat an experience that has been fulfilling the first time, but the theory and the practice can differ.

Occasionally, when past-life lovers meet again, circumstances have changed and they have nothing to learn from one another this lifetime. In such cases, the partners often find a deep initial attraction that rapidly fades, as their life paths pull them onward in different directions.

An example of this occurred with Oliver and Megan. They met and fell in love instantly, recognising one another immediately when they met. Upon meeting they both experienced a sense of recognition that arose from deep within, and Oliver was certain that they must have already met before in this lifetime. For days he puzzled over why he might feel instantly at home with someone who until recently was a complete stranger. Within weeks, however, they felt the tug of their life paths pulling them away from one another. It was a painful experience, but instinctively they knew that this was not the time for them to be together again.

Oliver's ambition for public life pushed him onwards toward his career goals whereas Megan was not interested in career, preferring family life instead. Oliver realised that if he pursued a long-term love relationship with Megan, he'd have to sacrifice his ambition for a simple life in the country. Megan realised, too, that staying with Oliver would mean that her plans for a close family living in the country were impossible, as he sought a corporate career which required that he live in a city. They were very much in love with one another and when in each other's company, their desires for their own life goals diminished. Despite this underlying attraction, partly based upon positive past-life experiences of love together, Oliver and Megan separated in order to pursue their paths this lifetime.

Agreeing to meet again does not guarantee that the next life shared will provide opportunities to master lessons together, but this explains why we sometimes fall in love and feel that the new partner is to be a life partner, only to watch the relationship fade and our plans fall apart. Sometimes intense beginnings to short-term love relationships are an indication of a past-life shared and an agreement to meet again.

Unless, however, there is a specific lesson to learn together or a shared path to tread, such relationships falter soon after you have fulfilled your agreement to meet again. Although this may be painful at the time, when you keep in mind the bigger picture of many lives and many loves, you may realise that the pursuit of a love relationship that will not further your spiritual growth is a hindrance rather than an opportunity.

In some cases, although you have more to learn together, this is not the lifetime in which to further your development together. It may be necessary to agree to meet again, after a brief meeting this lifetime to remind one another that you are still on the path to spiritual fulfilment. This occurred with Christopher and Ella, who were both in other relationships when they met and fell in love at a conference. Christopher's wife was about to give birth to their third child, and Ella was about to be married.

Realising the pain that such a relationship might cause to his wife and children, Christopher decided not to pursue the relationship with Ella, despite their intense feelings for one another. According to Christopher, they cried for almost two hours as they held one another on the sofa of their hotel room on the last day of the conference. Theirs was not an easy decision as Christopher still thinks of Ella regularly and the path not taken, although he is happy with his wife and children.

Those two hours spent holding one another is an example of Christopher and Ella's energetic agreement to meet again in order to pursue a love relationship. When the times arrives for them to meet again, they will have to determine once again if the circumstances are right for them to pursue a love relationship.

Had they left their partners and pursued a love relationship with the rationale that they were soul mates, they might have caused great pain to those around them and in turn they'd have to redress the issues arising from such actions at some later date. In such a case Christopher might experience a lifetime with his present wife where they are soul mates who have unfinished karma to re-balance. Denying their desires has caused Christopher and Ella pain but limited the suffering of those around them. If they are meant to be together then another opportunity will present itself; in this lifetime or in another. It could be argued that the pain they experience is the result of their limited viewpoint. If they were able to see the bigger picture (many lifetimes and the paths they are treading), their pain might subside. It may be necessary for them to master some spiritual lessons apart from those with one another, perhaps with other soul mates.

Sometimes life circumstances can appear to conspire to take us in directions that prevent a soul-mates love relationship from developing to its full potential. This can make it difficult to determine whether you are meant to pursue such a relationship or not.

An example of this occurred with a client of mine, Clarissa. In the closing months of World War II, Clarissa, who lived in England at the time, fell in love with an American soldier named Trevor. Her mother disapproved of any interaction between the two and soon Trevor was transferred home again but Clarissa was forbidden to contact him.

Clarissa married another man and moved to Australia. She told me that not one day had passed without her wondering about what might have been, had she pursued a love relationship with Trevor. Although she had three children and had since retired from work and pursued other interests, she still missed Trevor. She had separated from her husband and missed Trevor as though he had left very recently.

I suggested that she locate him in order to see if an opportunity lay ahead for them and she did. After several months of letters and phone calls, she found him and was amazed to be told that he had missed her, too, and that he had travelled around the world twice in search of her. He was planning another world trip that was to include Australia and they were reunited when he arrived some weeks later.

Clarissa and Trevor took an ocean cruise through the South Pacific to become re-acquainted and to catch up on lost years. Trevor had married, and his wife had died several years before, leaving him free to recall the love of his life.

I saw Clarissa two years later and asked her how it was going. She told me that despite strong feelings for one another, they had decided to return home to their respective countries as too many years had passed for them to make the relationship work. They each wanted to remain living in their own cities, as they wanted their families to be close, and Sydney and Seattle had proved too far away from each other for things to work.

Upon hearing this I was saddened, not for the fact that it wasn't being pursued but that they had taken almost 50 years to realise this. Fifty years is too long to spend with one partner whilst thinking about someone else.

Agreeing to disagree

In theory it's easy to agree to allow there to be differences between yourself and your relationship partner. After all, if you were both identical there'd be nothing interesting or exciting about being together.

In reality, much time and effort is sometimes spent trying to remove those attitudes, beliefs and characteristics that make your partner different from yourself, usually to no avail. In psychology it is sometimes referred to as the 'power struggle' stage of a relationship. This stage follows the first or the 'romantic stage' of love relationship. In the romantic stage of love you tend to see only the similarities you share with your partner. The power struggle stage that follows highlights the differences between partners and it involves them trying to control one another in order to have the relationship the way they'd like it to be.

What each of us eventually realises is that the power struggle stage is a 'no-win' situation. If you lose, you end up being controlled by your partner, and if you win, you end up turning your partner into someone that they're not, in which case they become distant, resentful or depressed. It's all part of attempting to have life on your terms and this rarely works for very long. This is not suggesting that you have to accept life on any terms, but some adaptability is recommended, especially in relationships. An example of this was Robina, who wanted to have a relationship with a man she admired.

Rick was the man Robina admired, but Rick was always working, in order to achieve the great heights to which he aspired. Friends often said to Robina, 'Oh, you must be so proud of Rick', and one night over dinner she'd had enough. 'If one more person tells me how proud of you I should be, I'll tell them about your bed wetting,' she stated for the whole table to hear. Rick blushed and then glared at her and we never heard another word about it.

When Robina decided that she wanted a man that she admired, she never considered how life might feel in the shadow of his achievements. After a few years the admiration wore thin, as she felt like an accessory to Rick and his achievements. When Robina decided to allow Rick to pursue his achievements, she felt free to allow herself the same privilege. Soon Robina was achieving her own goals and everyone was happy; for a while at least.

After the power struggle comes the negotiation, and in negotiation we find ways to meet all sorts of needs. Negotiation allows for the human needs as well as the needs of the spirit, but negotiation requires communication.

The respondents to the soul-mates questionnaire repeatedly listed communication as one of the most important lessons of their relationships, some even suggesting that their relationships only achieved their full potential after communication improved. Knowing how you best communicate and how your partner best communicates are important if you have any long-term plans for your relationship.

Communication isn't just about talking; for some people it involves being touched. A gentle back rub or a foot massage can mean more to some people than four hours of talking. For others listening is important, for we all need to be heard from time to time. It is amazing how much detail you can recall months after a conversation when you have truly listened to what the person said. When you are present in your body and all of you is listening, you anchor in your memory more detail than if you simply heard what was said.

Allowing your partner to hold opinions that differ from your own is the first step towards a tolerant love relationship. In a tolerant relationship it is often easier to reveal yourself without being afraid of being judged by your partner. This can allow for a deeper intimacy that benefits both partners. An example of developing tolerance occurred with a client named Doug when he attended a self-development weekend workshop and arrived feeling very nervous. To offset his nervousness, he scanned the room and mentally found fault with the other participants before having met them. Doug inwardly criticised them on the morning of the first day but by the afternoon his opinion of them had softened.

As each person laid their life open with a raw honesty he had not previously witnessed, Doug felt humbled to observe such courage. After the course concluded, Doug was given a ride home by another participant and on that long drive it occurred to him that where people are concerned perhaps most judgement is pre-judgement. Without a full awareness of a person's history, how can you accurately judge them? How can you know with certainty what has led a person to being who they are or to doing what they do?

When Doug arrived home, his new acquaintance helped him with his luggage and then embraced him with a big hug. Doug was dwarfed by this enormous bear of a man but he didn't care. He felt that this was important human contact, and after what they'd been through on the weekend, they needed it. As Doug waved him goodbye, he noticed a neighbour staring at them with a perplexed expression and he smiled. Without all the information (about the weekend of group activities that led to their hug on the footpath), she was forming an opinion short of all the facts.

Then Doug applied the attitude to his own relationship, realising that unless he knew with any certainty why his partner did what she did, then he was probably pre-judging her. This brings us directly back to communication. It is only through careful and respectful communication that we can hope to discover why people think and do the things they do, to us, with us and without us. With all the facts, we can step from pre-judgement to clarity of judgement.

Chapter Sixteen

WHAT DO YOU OFFER A SOUL MATE?

❦

IF YOU ARE TO BE ONE HALF OF A SOUL-MATE LOVE RELATIONSHIP, THEN ASK YOURSELF THIS. What do I offer a partner in relationship? Are you sought out for your sense of humour, your steadfast, reliable nature or your physique?

Do you enliven a dinner party or are you the soul of discretion when others confide in you? Sometimes partners notice qualities within us that we cannot see in ourselves, but if we are honest with ourselves, it's not hard to see what we can bring to a relationship.

Perhaps one of the greatest gifts you can offer your soul mate is to be actively pursuing your spiritual path in this lifetime. If you languish on your path, knowing what you need to do but procrastinating when it comes to acting on your beliefs, then you are in effect squandering another chance to develop spiritually. I say 'another chance' because doubtlessly we have all squandered some chances in the past.

Some might argue that too much intense spiritual work and no play makes life dull and tedious, but does all spiritual development have to be intense and dull? In following the path towards which you are best suited, you are often making headway along your spiritual path while in and between soul-mate love relationships, which can lighten the load of the relationship when it arrives.

On a more physical level, the questionnaire below examines the day-to-day part of a soul-mate love relationship, the actual relating. There's no point in feeling spiritually superior if your life is physically and emotionally a mess. The spiritual, mental, emotional and physical must all be kept in balance with one another for life to remain in harmony.

The following questionnaire is not only to establish what you bring to your relationships but to highlight what type of partner you are in love relationships. What you offer a relationship and what sort of relationship partner you become may be entirely different, as shown in the following example.

Chris is a sensitive, creative man and many women are attracted to him for his shy, soft nature. In relationships, however, Chris becomes jealous, possessive, demanding and at times dictatorial. He is a completely different person when in a relationship than with his friends. This is partly because Chris has a different set of rules for friendships than for his relationships. In friendships Chris has less invested emotionally and in turn he expects less of his friends. To his friends Chris appears to be easy-going and undemanding.

Because Chris invests much more of himself in his love relationships, he feels that he has more to lose and so he takes them much more seriously. So seriously, in fact, that he doesn't play with his partner the way he can play with his friends. His insecurities surface with his relationship partners, and in turn he shows his partners a side of him that his friends never get to see. When he feels insecure, Chris can become silently resentful, withdrawn and sullen and his partner can feel shut out emotionally.

If you were to ask his friends what Chris was like, they'd describe a completely different person to the one painted by his relationship partner. They'd both be right because they see different parts of Chris.

When completing the exercise below, please bear in mind how you are in love relationships and not in your friendships. Sometimes we have a different set of rules for how to behave in love compared to how to behave in a friendship. When answering these questions, think back to how you have been in previous love relationships, particularly your present or recent love relationships.

What do I offer a love relationship?

1. Are you honest about your thoughts and feelings with your partner?
2. Have your partners said that you were honest about your thoughts and feelings?
3. Are you supportive of your partner's plans such as career plans or personal goals?
4. Have your partners said that you were supportive of their plans?
5. Do you put your career or personal ambitions before your love relationship?
6. Have your partners suggested that you put your career or personal ambitions before a relationship?
7. Are you loyal to your relationship partner?
8. Do you lend a sense of order or structure to your relationships?
9. Do you lend a sense of passion and excitement to your relationships?
10. Are you spontaneous and adaptable to new circumstances?
11. How do you deal with financial issues with your relationship partner?

12. How do you resolve emotional issues with your partner?
13. How do you deal with those friends of your partner whom you dislike?
14. How do you share the everyday responsibilities with your partner such as paying bills, grocery shopping and cleaning the house?
15. Do you offer a more traditional approach to relationships, with more defined roles for each partner?
16. Do you offer a more modern approach to relationships, with less defined roles for each partner?
17. Are you open to negotiation with your partner regarding your sexual relationship with them?
18. Are you open to negotiation with your partner regarding decision making in your relationship?
19. Are you open to negotiation with your partner regarding finances?
20. Are you open to negotiating with your partner regarding shared responsibilities?
21. What do you perceive as your strengths in a relationship?
22. What do you perceive as your weaknesses in a relationship?

These are important issues because if you were to remove sex, money and control from relationships, you'd certainly reduce most of the arguments that disrupt the even flow of love relationships. In some cases sex, money and control are interwoven, making intimacy a minefield for the people involved. Take the case of Tom and Sandra, whose traditional relationship was set to explode when Sandra took a job.

As the primary breadwinner, Tom had a sense of pride in being able to provide for a family, and in return he liked to have things at home the way he preferred. Because Sandra relied on Tom for financial support and for a sense of structure, she went along with what Tom wanted, including having sex at his insistence on almost every day of their 25-year marriage.

When the children left school, Sandra felt that she had concluded her role as a mother, so she set about educating herself, preparing to re-enter the workforce. Tom felt insecure about this and discouraged her, telling her that she'd never pass her exams and that it was a lot tougher out there than it used to be. Sandra wavered and was about to give up her studies when her sister urged her to complete them, even if she was never to use them. For the sake of her own confidence, Sandra was encouraged to complete her studies.

Sandra completed her studies and then started working. With a new source of income, Sandra didn't need to rely on Tom as much as before and this left Tom feeling less needed. In a few months Sandra was less inclined to accept Tom's need for sex every day, especially after putting in a long day at work, and soon arguments flared over money and sex. They were becoming locked in a power struggle for the direction of their relationship.

Tom wanted things to be as they had always been for him, whereas Sandra felt that she had outgrown her role as a mother and provider for Tom. They appeared to have two basic possibilities:

1. They could negotiate a new direction for their relationship, with a new role for each of them that met each partner's needs (once they had identified those needs).
2. They could agree to go in different directions as they were unable to continue to meet their needs in their relationship.

Tom didn't want to separate and insisted that Sandra would be happy once she settled into her old role as mother and provider again. He even suggested that she have another child, and she baulked at this suggestion. Sandra had been given a taste of freedom and a new life and she wasn't going back to her old role for anything. She boldly told Tom that she wasn't interested in having sex with him again as he'd had more than his fair share with her for this lifetime.

This couple were about to find a completely new direction for their relationship, or they would simply separate and pursue different directions.

'What was so wrong with the life we had?' asked Tom.

'You're such a dinosaur, Tom. You were born in the wrong century. Where do you think you'll find a woman in this day and age who'll keep the house clean and happily have sex with you every day of the year? To be honest Tom, it was the most boring 12 minutes of every day.'

It became apparent that during the time that Tom had the sole income, he had complete control over their relationship. When Sandra secured her own income, she increased her choices and her opportunities. She also increased her power in their relationship, making her Tom's equal, probably for the first time.

Tom's perception was that he provided security and stability, yet in Sandra's view he was demanding, stubborn and old-fashioned. To soften Sandra's view and to help Tom to see that he wasn't redundant in the relationship, I asked Sandra what good things Tom still offered her.

She replied that he was honest, faithful and reliable, although she said that she now wanted someone more exciting and less reliable. Tom heard this and I pointed out to him that if things didn't work out with Sandra, there would be other women seeking an honest, reliable and faithful man for a love relationship. It wasn't what he wanted to hear at the time, but I knew that it was a seed planted in his mind for later, should he need to review what he had to offer another woman.

I then asked Tom what good things Sandra still offered him, even though she was independent now and unwilling to have a sexual relationship with him. Tom replied that although she had become more argumentative lately, she was still kind to him, and that she still managed to take time out to deal with the children's problems when they arose. He pointed out that although she wasn't able to stay home and maintain the house any more, she had arranged for a cleaner to come in once a week to keep the place clean and homely.

Tom watched as Sandra grew into her full potential and began to leave him behind. When one partner grows and develops at a rapid rate and the other stagnates, preferring to keep life as they know it, relationships are sorely tested. Tom saw that their roles in the relationship were changing and this presented opportunities as well as challenges. One possibility was that Tom could take on the passive role in the relationship and retire or cut back to part-time work, allowing Sandra to embrace the role she seemed so keen to pursue, but he wasn't interested.

I asked Sandra if she saw a role reversal as a possibility and she, too, seemed disinclined to pursue such a path. They had outgrown one another, possibly due to not negotiating their needs long ago.

Knowing what you can offer a love relationship can help you to know who suits you. There is no point having a droll, understated sense of humour when your partner prefers a lightning quick repartee, just as composing delicate poetry for someone whose idea of romance is a quick grope in a parked car is likely to end in disappointment.

An example of a lack of suitability occurred with a friend of mine, Angus. Being a romantic at heart, he arose early one morning and crept downstairs to the kitchen where he drew a large heart and the words 'I love you' in Rice Bubbles on the kitchen floor for his partner to discover when she awoke later. Shirley discovered the love message and in turn left a note for Angus saying 'You can clean it up.'

Angus was happy to find a dozen unusual ways to tell Shirley that he loved her but Shirley wanted him to tell her in the more traditional ways – a candlelight dinner and a dozen red roses. It finally occurred to Angus to seek out a partner who shared his eccentric perspective of life so that what he offered a partner might be appreciated.

It is essential that you are honest with yourself when completing the previous exercise, as your perceptions of yourself may differ greatly from how others perceive you. An example is Tony and Carol. Tony felt that he was sensitive whereas Carol described him as moody. When Carol felt that she was being honest with Tony, he felt that she was being brutal. This confirmed to him that he was indeed sensitive, whereas

Carol was then given to rolling her eyes and calling him 'a girl'.

This is why you are asked not only to think about how you see yourself, but also how others have perceived you in the past. If several previous partners have voiced the opinion that you are lazy and disorganised, then consider the possibility that they were correct.

An example of how you can misunderstand your life occurred many years ago when a friend named Toby sat with me by a roaring fire, sipping a drink and staring into the flames. After a long period of relaxed silence he spoke.

'You know, it's the simple things that make life worth living. Wouldn't you say?'

'Yes,' I replied, keeping an eye on a log that was determined to leap out of the grate onto the hearth rug.

'I'm glad to have such a simple life really,' he sighed and I burst into laughter, spilling my drink as I did so.

'But you don't have a simple life,' I said.

'How's that?'

'You run a business with 65 staff, you're always flying off to meetings, rushing around like the end of the world is nigh, and how does an imported sports car and a three-storey house fit into the simple life?'

'Well, I mean simple in that it's not as complicated as it used to be.'

'It was worse than this?' I gasped.

Although Toby was convinced that he was living a simple life, the average person might be excused for having given up on Toby's complicated life long ago. If, in filling out the previous questionnaire, you find that several of your past partners have disagreed with your view of yourself, perhaps it is time to reassess your opinion of yourself in relationships.

Being soul mates is no guarantee of a contented, uncomplicated relationship, in fact if anything it's probably the reverse. When couples come together to learn spiritual lessons, it is only human nature to try to impose your way of life onto your partner, and the result is pain in the learning of a lesson. That's not to suggest that the joy doesn't outweigh the pain, but that sometimes we need to be well clear of the relationship and the pain before we can weigh the joy and the pain with a balanced eye.

By keeping life's bigger picture in mind we are able to approach our spiritual lessons with anticipation, whereas when we lose sight of the bigger picture, we often have to be dragged, kicking and screaming toward those things we need to learn. An example of this occurred with Fiona and Louis. Fiona wanted a simple, ordered life, which surprised me, as she picked Louis to settle with. Louis wanted to change the world and to this end he spent many weeks of each year in Eastern Europe, Africa and Asia, setting up self-sufficient communities among the poverty-stricken. This kept Fiona and Louis apart for more than six months of every year and when she consulted me, Fiona was at the end of her tether. She wanted Louis to spend more time at home with her and yet he wanted to spend more time overseas, doing what he loved to do. When I asked Fiona if she thought that there was a future in their relationship with them having such different needs, she refused to countenance any thought of separation.

I delved deeper to see what their lesson was in this situation and it appeared to be to allow each other the space necessary to fulfil their destiny. When Louis was away Fiona felt insecure, whereas when he was at home he felt that he wasn't doing enough for those communities he was supporting. This couple was opposite in their day-to-day living, but their complementary approach to life was what had initially appealed to each of them. When I suggested that they might spend more time together if Fiona travelled with Louis to foreign countries she shuddered at the suggestion. I realised that she found poorer countries distasteful and disorganised.

When I suggested that they spend more time together at home in a way that helped Louis to feel like he was still contributing, her eyes narrowed slightly and she told me that was what she'd been trying to do for several months. I had the distinct impression that she was seeking a way to harness Louis, and I was unable to show her that in doing so, she risked losing him for the rest of this lifetime.

Louis wanted a dynamic partner to accompany him to wild and underdeveloped countries, to be at the cutting edge of community building, whereas Fiona wanted a practical, sensible man who knew the value of hard work and the steady accumulation of wealth and security. At a glance they appeared to be mismatched, but soul mates are together to learn lessons, and so they often have to abandon habits and the hope of a simple, stable life, in order to master a lesson contained within the relationship.

In the short term there is discomfort but in the longer term (many lifetimes) there is understanding. My final suggestion to Fiona was to remain the same until she no longer wanted to do so. That is, when she'd had enough of trying to go in a direction she believed might fulfil her, she might consider going where the ride was at first uncomfortable. If you resist life for too long, stagnation results and you eventually find yourself wishing for change.

Chapter Seventeen

PREPARING TO BE WITH YOUR SOUL MATE

IT SEEMS THAT ALMOST EVERYONE IS KEEN TO MEET AND TO BE WITH THEIR SOUL MATE IN A LOVE RELATIONSHIP BUT ONLY A FEW OF THOSE SEARCHING ACTUALLY KNOW HOW TO GO ABOUT FINDING THAT SPECIAL PERSON.

When we set out to find our soul mate, we are often, in fact, seeking a relationship partner, and soul mates frequently arrive when you are ready for the lessons. This chapter shows some techniques for preparing for a new love relationship, whether or not it be a soul-mate relationship.

There are three steps to help you locate your soul mate or partner who suits you:

1. Identifying what you want in a soul-mate partner.
2. Making yourself available for a soul-mate love relationship.
3. Asking for what you want.

These steps appear to be simple and straightforward, but when you consider how many people want to be with their soul mate and yet remain unhappily single, it cannot be as simple as it first appears.

As you complete the following exercises, it is essential that you are brutally honest with yourself. If you don't want others to see your details, use your own paper and burn it afterwards to maintain your privacy. Knowing that you'll be burning the information afterwards may help you to be more honest.

If you're not prepared to be totally honest with yourself, you cannot expect a partner to be honest with you, nor can you expect to find someone who will actually fulfil you. The perfect love relationship may not be the perfect love relationship for you. Forget about what other people might think and instead think about how good you'll feel when you're with the person who is best suited to your current spiritual path.

Step 1. Identifying what you want in a soul-mate partner. Tick below the basic requirements you desire in a partner.

Gender	Health
Age group	Interests
Single	Sensual
Available	Cerebral
Colouring	Reflective
Height	Tactful
Weight	Straightforward
Build	Sociable
Wants to have children	Aloof
Already has children	Financially conservative
Doesn't want children	Financially adventurous
Temperament	Financially stable
Type of sense of humour	Bohemian
Location	Creative

Artistic	Atheist
Musical	Agnostic
A good cook	Generous
Multilingual	Enthusiastic
Open-minded	Reliable
Religious	Likes routine
Spiritually aware	Other

There are two schools of thought surrounding the act of identifying your needs and asking the universe to meet those needs. The first belief is that it is essential that you make it known that you are ready for what you seek and that you prepare yourself for the imminent arrival of your desired partner.

By concentrating on yourself and your own readiness, you are in fact creating a vacuum, which the universe will seek to fill. This approach involves making room for your new partner and becoming aware of your surroundings as life attempts to meet your needs. The simple steps for this method are outlined below.

1. Review your previous love relationships, identifying the qualities you want in a new partner. Concentrate only on what you want, not what you don't want.
2. Examine your present circumstances to determine whether you are single, available and keen to pursue a new love relationship. If not, then you may need to take steps to become single and available and open to a new love relationship.
3. When you have completed Step 2, tell the universe or God that you are ready for a new love relationship and that you'll gladly accept the perfect person for you at this stage of your life.

There is no point asking for the perfect person, as we are all imperfect if judged critically. Also, if you receive someone who you feel is perfect, you may feel that you are not equal to your partner, creating problems in your ability to give or receive love.

The perfect person for you now may be entirely different to your preconceptions, yet if that person furthers your spiritual growth and your ability to love and to be loved in return, then they are perfect for you. What is the point of the previous exercise, you might well ask. The previous technique works for some people and the slightly more involved exercise below works for others. The technique is not as important as the outcome. If one of them works for you, then all well and good.

Recently a client of mine told me that she successfully used the following technique to find a partner. As she kept her eyes open for a new man, a woman arrived and they fell in love. She told me that she was surprised but that she's never felt happier and more loved in her life. I'm inclined to agree that if your needs are being met and no one is being hurt or damaged in any way, then accepting the love that life is offering you is probably the best step you can take. Had this woman made a detailed list of her perfect partner, she might have missed her opportunity for love by narrowing her focus of attention.

Are you single and or available for a soul-mate love relationship?

If not, what do you need to do to become single or available?

When you feel that you are ready, willing and able to enjoy a soul-mate love relationship, state aloud that you are. For example, 'I am now ready to accept the perfect love relationship for me at this time.'

When you have stated aloud that you are ready for your soul mate, forget about searching and allow life to deliver them to you. If you keep asking, you cannot receive. Ask and then divert your attention to other things while life fulfils your request for a soul-mate partner.

A second school of thought involves reflecting upon your past patterns in relationships, in order to decide what qualities you seek in your next partner. If you don't drink alcohol, for example, it may be unwise for you to partner with someone who likes a bottle of red wine with dinner five nights a week. On the other hand, if you enjoy reading books, partnering with an outdoors/adventurous type might suit you, as you'll be left alone to read as your partner climbs another mountain.

Some people find this method too exacting and tedious, whereas others need this method in order to clearly identify the type of person that might suit them. This second method involves four basic steps:

1. Review your previous love relationships in order to determine what you liked and didn't like, so as to better prepare your list of what you want in a new partner.
2. Examine your present circumstances to determine whether you are single, available and keen to pursue a new love relationship.
3. Prepare a list of the desired qualities you seek in a partner and write down when you'd like that relationship to commence, for example, soon, after Christmas, next year or right now.
4. Ask for it. Ask the universe aloud for your soul-mate partner.

In discussing the writing of this book over lunch with a friend recently, she grew excited by the possibility of finding a new partner, having been single for nearly nine years.

'There are no good men living around here,' she stated as she poured a glass of wine.

'In a city of four million people you're telling me that you cannot find one suitable man?' I laughed.

'Well you show me one then,' she said pointedly.

I might have known then that she didn't really want a man but preferred to give the impression that she was still looking for love. There's something to be said for having your life exactly the way you want it to be. Your towel can take up the whole towel rail, and you can be safe in the knowledge that no-one else will eat the last of your favourite yoghurt in the refrigerator. All your furniture is placed exactly where you want it to be and you can decorate as you please. Sometimes it is easier to stay in your comfortable routines than to make changes that might require effort. There's nothing quite like other people to sharpen your focus.

Instead of heeding my intuition over my lunchtime friend, I suggested that she place a free advertisement in the personal columns on the Internet. I even offered to write her ad if she supplied a small colour photograph of herself. Two hours later I had written three ads and she selected the one which made her laugh the most, and after handing me the photo, it was confirmed. I returned home and placed the ad and photo on an Internet site and within a week she had several responses.

The following week I telephoned to see how things were going and she was unenthusiastic.

'Yes, I've had a few responses, but you should see what they look like.'

'And have you written to anyone to see what they write like?' I asked.

'No. No-one appeals to me.'

It was then that I realised that she wasn't really interested in a love relationship, and that I was doing all the work. She was simply finding new people to criticise and reject without making any effort to get to know them. As a courtesy to those who had responded, I asked my friend to write each of them a short note, and I told her that I'd cancel her ad. It was unfair to advertise herself as available when she was clearly not interested in starting a new relationship.

In my enthusiasm I had jumped over Step 2 and completed Step 3 in the above process. If I had completed Step 2, I'd have realised that my friend was not available for a love relationship, and I needn't have written an ad for her or listed it on the Internet. Often I find clients who are engrossed in the process of making a list for their perfect partner, and while this is an exciting exercise, if you are not yet ready for love, it is a waste of time. Several years after a long-term relationship ended, I found myself still single and I sat down to ask myself why. I couldn't find a reason, but when I imagined myself sharing my life and my home with someone new, I grew resistant and stubborn with the thought. I realised that I was not ready for another relationship as my thoughts turned to those things I'd have to give up when sharing with another person, instead of imagining those things I'd gain by being with someone new.

There is nothing wrong with choosing to be single, especially if you enjoy yourself. It's when you believe that you want a new relationship but have an emotional resistance to such a goal that problems arise.

An example of this occurred with Natasha. A few months ago, Natasha and her friend Holly sat down one evening and made lists of their ideal partners, and asked for partners to present themselves. Both single and available, the women knew that it was a simple task of identifying what they wanted, listing those qualities and asking the universe for their perfect men. Their lists are included below.

Three months later Holly has her perfect man and Natasha is still single and available. At first I was puzzled as to why the universe had answered the request of one person and not the other, when they had asked for their desired partners on the same day. I decided to examine Natasha's list.

Natasha's list

'The partner I would like to meet and be with very soon, if it is for my highest good and in accordance with the divine, will be:
- available now, physically, emotionally and psychologically;
- a man; not gay nor bisexual
- warm-hearted, kind, generous, sweet
- loving, affectionate, tender
- sensual and sexual

- able to receive, understand and accept me as I am – a mother with a less than perfect body
- able to communicate his thoughts, feelings, needs, wants and heart's desires
- light-hearted, optimistic, cheerful and not moody, pessimistic or bitter
- fun-loving, playful and ready to go, adaptable, resourceful and competent
- he loves the kind of music I do
- talented and successful
- creative, but not in an art form I'm not interested in
- healthy, vital and vibrant and not frenzied, agitated or nervous
- a brilliant mind
- a sensational wit
- rich so that we can travel and give money away and be generous
- have a beautiful house in a beautiful place near to my mother
- a nature lover and enjoys walking, hiking, flowers, trees, birds, beauty, travelling but not to the Philippines or places I don't like – instead to places that interest me
- already have a fitted out campervan with two fantastic sleeping bags that zip together
- marvellous company and conversational at all times of the night or day
- have a beautiful voice, dry palms and feet, and smells divine;
- his touch is warm
- his breath is beautiful
- he doesn't snore
- he doesn't burp or fart too much or pick his nose
- I like his taste in clothing and aesthetic objects
- I like his values and opinions
- I have confidence in him, and I trust and respect him
- he is in touch with his spirit and has attained wisdom and is not into any wanky cult or belief but is grounded in spirit directly and lives it in his daily life
- he eats and drinks similar things to me and enjoys them
- he doesn't smoke or get drunk

- he doesn't take drugs or gamble
- he doesn't lie but is not a prissy prune-arse and knows how to do things moderately and have a good time
- he is authentic to himself, tolerant, obliging, observant, whimsical, fanciful and charms me
- he likes films I like and doesn't make me go to dreadful, tedious plays or irritating sports fixtures
- he can help me in my life with things I'm not good at e.g. tidying my desk, tidying my CDs and tapes and videos, cleaning, organising, putting up shelves and fixing things
- he can cook delicious things
- he can look after me reciprocally
- we can nurture, benefit and enhance each other
- we bring out the best in each other
- we don't fight but instead resolve our issues easily and generously
- we are comrades, soul mates, cut from the same cloth, sharing the same vibration
- we laugh a lot together and we can also cry together
- we kiss and touch each other all the time
- we make light of difficulties and find solutions together easily
- we are survivors
- we are very well suited to common enterprises and we work happily and effectively together to benefit ourselves and all beings
- we find each other beautiful, desirable, captivating and compelling
- he is not interested in other women at all and thinks he's absolutely blessed to be with me and thanks his lucky stars
- he chooses to be with me and seeks out my company without being confining
- I feel free to be myself with him
- I feel free and supported to be truly authentic
- I never feel like I'm selling myself out when I'm with him
- he has nice writing, sloping to the right
- he opens the door to a world I'd like to inhabit

- I love his world, his friends, his family, his essence, his habits and his particular way.

When I first read this list I saw two possible partners – the Dalai Lama or God, opening the door to a world Natasha would like to inhabit. It is most definitely a specific list and I'm sure Natasha would add more to it, given the chance. As I write this, Natasha is still single.

I spoke with Natasha several times after she composed this list and one thing that she didn't list but which stood out to me was that she was tired of love relationships that started out with promise and slowly faded. In short, she wanted a love that was to last forever. It's not an uncommon desire among people seeking soul-mate love relationships, but the odds against someone coming into your life and growing in the same direction as yourself and at the same pace as you are unbelievably high. That's not to say impossible, but undoubtedly something few of us would bet on if they were odds in a horse race or a lottery. Yet despite these incredibly high odds, many of us still believe that there is someone out there who will play Romeo to our Juliet and some of us are silently holding our breath in the hope of the imminent arrival of our prince or princess.

In making the above list, Natasha was outlining to herself exactly the type of man she wanted. This would help her to recognise him when he approached her, and writing it gave her a chance to revise the list at a later date if necessary.

Each quality on the list must be re-read carefully in order for you to ask yourself if you'd actually enjoy being with someone who has the qualities you have listed. Most people argue that they'd only list things that they desire so it would pointless reviewing the list but I disagree. Sometimes how we perceive ourselves is not how we actually are. I can still recall a past partner's riotous laughter after I told her how I'd love to renovate an old house myself. 'You can't even buy a pair of jeans that fit, so how on earth could you order carpet for a room?' she asked. I perceived myself as a practical guy whereas she perceived me as impractical.

When I made a mental or a physical list of qualities I desired in a partner, the words 'independent' and 'adventurous' usually cropped up. One day I had to own up to the fact that I am neither independent nor adventurous and being with a partner who has those qualities is uncomfortable for me. The more I examined my lists, the more convinced I became that I didn't really know the sort of partner to which I was best suited, and that leaving it all up to God or the universe couldn't be any worse than my own judgement. That isn't to say that my relationships were disastrous, but only that I felt that I was cramping my partner's style by being so sensitive and unadventurous.

So instead of making a list, I simply told the universe when I was ready to love again, and often a partner arrived who was different from my previous partners.

Natasha's friend Holly also wrote a list.

Holly's List

My future partner, who I want very soon in my life, if it is for my highest good and in accordance with the divine, will be:

- a loving, accepting, heterosexual – a great heart
- comfortable with himself
- emotionally stable
- unafraid to love with intimacy
- has a strong sense of his spirituality
- emotionally unattached
- 52 to 60 years of age
- is artistic or generally appreciates the arts
- good sense of humour
- has divine loves
- good body – with beautiful lips, good-sized penis and good bum
- intelligent
- pleasant, interesting face
- able to be spontaneous, playful
- adores me – loves me unconditionally
- financially secure, with his own house

- has been in long relationships before
- grown-up children whom I love and who love my own children
- adventurous/will love to travel with me
- interesting occupation but not consumed by it
- healthy – non-smoker – though not rigid in habits
- looks after himself
- enjoys reading, music, arts, sex, talking, socialising, meditating, exploring, trying new adventures
- generous and comfortable with money
- adores discussing ideas of awareness and spirituality
- really notices things in a loving, curious way
- is independent, allowing me to also enjoy my independence
- non-possessive
- good listener
- great cook – creative and healthy
- divine dancer
- gets on well with my friends
- loves beauty and funny, quirky incidences and things
- versatile, flexible and able to adapt to change of situation no matter how strange
- warmly assertive and clear about his needs and boundaries
- loves to communicate and will work through problems and is unafraid to face them
- interesting dresser and appreciates my style
- up for new ideas
- creative thinker
- imaginative
- has faced his demons, so loving and compassionate to those who are suffering
- interested in the environment, politics and working in the world
- has wide interests in many aspects of life

It is a slightly shorter list than Natasha's, but specific nonetheless. Soon after making this list, Holly started a love relationship. When I looked for the differences in the lists, I found that each had her own level of readiness for a love relationship. Holly was eager for a new relationship whereas Natasha seemed somewhat jaded by life and all the possible complications a new love relationship might present. You do need to ask yourself if you are ready for a new love relationship, and before you answer that question with your mind, listen to the reaction within your body. Your body will tell you if you are comfortable with the idea of a new relationship.

Natasha described a relationship workshop she attended several years ago in which they were asked to make a list of exactly what they wanted in a partner. When they had completed this exercise, the instructor asked them to carefully scrutinise their lists, and to become aware that everything on their lists was keeping them from having a great relationship.

In effect, he argued that their desires for particular qualities in a relationship partner prevented them from seeing opportunities which life offered them. This is a valid point, as it is easy to become lost in the 'fine print' and lose sight of the overall.

If we were to distil our needs for the perfect love relationship down to one sentence, many of us might simply want to be loved and understood by another person. These are simple, basic human needs and all the physical attributes many people list are a complicated way of saying how they want to be loved and understood.

Another, somewhat simpler technique is to ready yourself for love and to allow it to find you. In readying yourself you have to remember that you are probably on someone else's wish list so preparation is likely to make the lift-off easier. At the risk of being repetitive, becoming ready for love is more than half the challenge. Over and over again I hear how people are ready but how love seems to avoid them. When I hear this I ignore the words and scan their energy. It doesn't take long to find the real resistance, whether it be fear, pain or a wall protecting them from being loved again after a deep and painful loss. A detailed list is designed to help you become accustomed to the idea of a new love relationship, but at the same time the list may presume that the universe doesn't know what is best for you in relationships. Sometimes it helps to pen a detailed list to clarify your desires, whereas at other times it's best to simply ask the universe for the perfect partner for you at present without being specific at all.

Finding your soul group

If you extend the understanding of soul mates being those who have shared past lives with us, it makes sense that beyond the friendships and love relationships of soul mates, each of us has a soul group. This is a group of souls who have shared experiences and have a common perspective on life. This group of souls may have entered human life experience at the same time in history, or they may have shared experiences and as a result, share a similar life perspective.

When you spend time with your soul group, you have a sense of finding your true family. This is your spiritual family. Although you may not share all of their beliefs, your history together allows for a sense of unity. Perhaps your soul group centres around a religion or a set of philosophic beliefs, even beliefs which are different to those you were raised with.

An example of this is Samantha, whose soul group is a wide variety of musicians and entertainers. When among people who allow her to be as passionate about life as she wants to be, Samantha feels at home. When among those who don't understand her, Samantha closes up like a flower.

Your soul group may not even be found in the country of your origin and when you do locate them, they may be scattered far and wide across the globe. They may have a lifestyle or a career at odds with your own and yet still share your viewpoint of life. An example of this occurred many years ago when the husband of a student arrived to meet his wife after a tarot class and we started talking. He was an engineer and we became so engrossed in a conversation about physics and engineering that his wife literally had to take him by the arm to get him to finish our conversation and leave with her.

When you first contact someone from your soul group, you'll feel distinctly at ease, and you'll be glad to share your thoughts without having to edit them according to how they may be wrongly perceived. From time to time I share an evening with some people from my soul group doing what we love best – making music.

Over the years, some of us have become professional musicians while others still play solely for enjoyment. An assortment of instruments including a piano, saxophones, drum kit, guitars and a ukelele make for a night of noisy revelry, fuelled by endless margaritas and the occasional cigar. Our first recording was entitled 'Songs in No Particular Key' and it was an example of accuracy in labelling.

When you find your soul group it doesn't matter what you do together, as you'll be enjoying one another's company. For those wanting to locate their soul group, consider attending some spiritual talks and demonstrations until you find what 'clicks for you'. There are many opportunities such as the talks and demonstrations given by the Theosophical Society, which has branches worldwide. Their talks include introductions to a wide variety of spiritual paths, methods of divination and meditations, which may be attended by those who share your spiritual purpose.

Some people stumble upon their soul group by accident, whereas others locate those who share their spiritual path after a long and careful search. By actively seeking out new experiences, especially group activities, you'll be increasing your chances of meeting those in your soul group. Your soul group is a part of your spiritual family.

One client of mine stumbled across his soul group one evening when he went out to a hotel to meet his co-tenant, Suzanne. Nathan took down the wrong name for the meeting point (a hotel in the inner city), and ended up three streets away from Suzanne. While she waited patiently in the beer garden of the Royal Oak Hotel, Nathan was drawing the attention of several men in the Oak and Thistle, a gay bar and bistro. Lifelong friendships were started that evening for Nathan, unfortunately at some cost to his ongoing friendship with Suzanne, who was furious at being stood up.

It can be depressing to observe someone who insists upon fitting in with people who don't understand or appreciate them. An accountant in the circus or a juggler in a bank is the analogy I use to illustrate what it feels like to those who cling to a family or to a circle of friends because that is all they know. Your jokes are ignored or misunderstood, and your creative attempts are derided or remain unvalued by those close to you. Life is too short to squander it among people who don't appreciate you. Those in your soul group will know instinctively where you are in life and share many of your perspectives and interests.

Colin learned this the hard way in his early twenties, having a group of friends who tolerated instead of appreciating him. Colin often wrote long letters to these friends in order to cheer them up or to share his thoughts with them. One day it occurred to him that if he never wrote to these people again, he wouldn't be missed. Years later, when he was writing for magazines, the friends who had not missed him decided that what he had to say suddenly had merit simply because others were happy to pay for his words.

It was then that Colin chose to seek out his soul group. Over the next two years he observed which friendships took more from him than they offered, and he thinned out his friends and acquaintances. Next he decided to be open to new interests, avenues and opportunities, and before he could blink, he was overwhelmed by offers and opportunities. Courses, parties, creative and sporting get-togethers and support for his plans materialised almost immediately and he hasn't looked back, except to remind himself what life was like when he chose to remain with those who didn't share his path in life.

Although life isn't always a party, it doesn't have to be a continual struggle, alone and misunderstood by those closest to you. Your physical family are not necessarily your soul group. You may have one parent, or a brother or sister, who shares your spiritual life perspective but part of the journey involves finding the rest of your soul group currently in physical bodies around the world.

Chapter Eighteen

THE SOUL MATES EXCUSE

SOME PEOPLE FIND IT NECESSARY TO USE THE TERM 'SOUL MATE' AS AN EXCUSE FOR BAD BEHAVIOUR IN RELATIONSHIPS, BUT TREATING OTHERS BADLY HAS ITS OWN RESULTS, REGARDLESS OF ANY PAST LIVES OR PRESENT SPIRITUAL PURPOSE SHARED. An example of this occurred with Claudia. When I asked her why she had left her two young children with her husband to pursue a new life with Adrian, she explained to me that it was because she and Adrian were soul mates.

'But if you perceive soul mates as those with whom you have outstanding lessons to learn, don't you feel that leaving your children behind will only call you back to those souls at some later date, in order to complete the lessons you have started with them this lifetime?' I asked her.

'Perhaps, but my lesson with Adrian was urgent and I knew that we had only one chance to learn it. This was our chance. Don't you see?'

'And how is your relationship with Adrian developing?'

'Oh, not so well.'

'Why?'

'He wants to start a family but he doesn't think I'm the right person to do that with.'

'Why?'

'He thinks I'll leave the kids behind if someone new comes along.'

'And would you?'

'No. I've tried to explain to him that he was the exception to the rule but he won't believe me.'

'I can see his point.'

'Then why is it that when a man leaves his children for another woman it is perfectly acceptable, yet when a woman leaves her children for another man it is a scandal?'

'You have a point there. So what exactly was the lesson that Adrian offered you that was so urgent?'

'Adrian was successful and he offered me a life my husband couldn't offer.'

'What sort of life exactly?'

'He offered me an imported new car, a job in his company and overseas trips where we had enough time to indulge ourselves and relax. With my husband it was all work and no appreciation.'

'I can see how many people would want the life you've described that Adrian offered you, especially when compared with the life you had with your husband, but how is exchanging family life for financial independence a spiritual lesson?'

'I guess you had to be there to understand it all,' she sighed.

'I guess so,' I echoed.

It is hard to accurately judge from the outside why people do some of the things they do in life, but that in itself is not enough to accept that all actions can be justified by the claim that the person desired was a soul mate. Sometimes the term 'soul mate' is simply a justification for actions, in order to lend spiritual respectability to those actions. The reverse of this might be the claim that 'the devil made me do it'.

Or as a seven-year-old boy might ask: 'Mummy, do all men in their forties meet young soul mates soon after they've bought shiny new sports cars?'

'Well, not all men, but most. And you can look forward to a new sports car and a new girlfriend when you turn 45, too, sweetheart.'

In another case, a client named Benson kept a mistress in an apartment in the centre of town for 13 years while keeping it secret from his wife and family. His justification was that they were soul mates but that he couldn't forsake his obligations to his family. Meanwhile his wife was not free to pursue her own life and to seek a more committed love relationship, and his children were observing role models who went through the motions of being in a love relationship without actually being emotionally present. When the situation finally went sour, the mistress was given the apartment Benson had paid for but his wife had to fight for her share of the family home.

Soul mate or family pattern?

When meeting a partner with whom you share a similar history, it can feel like meeting a soul mate, as your steps have paired despite having never previously met. If, for example, you were left with great responsibilities for family members as a child and you met a partner with a similar family history, chances are you'd feel a bond of understanding, due to having both been given responsibilities at an early age.

Although these historical patterns can create a sense of familiarity between partners, this is not confirmation that you are soul mates. Such a shared history may help strengthen a love relationship if the shared history is positive.

In his book *Families and How to Survive Them*, psychiatrist Robin Skynner details an exercise with several dozen therapists who are strangers in a large room. They are asked to pair off with someone else in the room, but not to talk while doing so. That is, they have to pair off with someone without the aid of verbal communication.

After everyone had paired off, they were asked to find out what they had in common, and sure enough, almost everyone in the room had paired off with someone who shared some of their own history. This suggested that in seeking a partner we use non-verbal clues to identify who shares our history and who might better understand us.

Soul mates and those who are in relationships because they share similar goals can both have long and fulfilling love relationships. The difference is that those who choose to be together without being soul mates don't have life pushing them towards particular spiritual lessons. Theirs may be a less stressful relationship, depending on the personalities involved and the circumstances.

The initial attraction for someone who shares your present-life emotional history may feel like a soul mates connection because you have so much in common, and it may be every bit as rewarding in the long term, but it is not necessarily a soul-mates love relationship. A soul-mate relationship implies some past-life history shared and not just present-life similarities in upbringing or experiences. Although you may well share steps on your spiritual paths that benefit you both and result in your becoming soul mates, you were not soul mates when you met, simply by having similarities in your life to date. If you're happy and content to be together, then the difference does not matter.

A shared history is a powerful bonding force, as shown with Carlos and Marguerite, who shared a similar history. Both had grown up in poverty in South America among large families, and they both had to leave school early to work in order to provide for younger siblings. When they met in Australia, it was as though they had finally found their 'other halves'. They worked two jobs each for the first six years together, saving in order to purchase a small house. Then they saved for a business and 27 years after starting out with a large mortgage and a business dream, they own the business premises and three properties, including a small farm where Carlos dreams of retiring to grow grapes and to make his own wine.

In the 35 years that the have been together, Marguerite and Carlos have rarely argued, as they share the same life perspective. They admire one another's ability to work hard for desired goals, and they both have strong family values. Two of their three children run the business these days, as Marguerite gently reminds Carlos that they are older now, and that grapevines and a large garden beckons. A positive similar history in this lifetime can be a powerful stabiliser in love relationships, especially when upheavals threaten the stability of the relationship.

Both Carlos and Marguerite shared the same practical application to their plans, and rather than collapse when life thwarted their plans, they pondered another approach and never tired of applying themselves to their shared goals. Carlos appreciated Marguerite's lack of pretension and simple contentment with life's routines and in turn she shared his dream of living in the country with a vegetable garden and a few animals, like they had both grown up with in South America. Through sharing many years together this lifetime, Carlos and Marguerite are on a spiritual journey together, and this now makes them soul mates, for if they should meet one another again in a future life, they may recall their rewarding experiences shared in this lifetime. This is likely to help them to bond when they meet again.

But some history shared can lead to destructive behaviour patterns in relationships, and sometimes partners still remain together because it feels natural to them to do so. Growing up with alcoholic parents and then pairing with an alcoholic may feel natural or familiar, but it is not necessarily a soul-mate relationship nor will it necessarily further your spiritual development. Sometimes it is simply a case of repeating what you grew up with.

Determining the difference between a soul-mates connection and the initial rush of recognition that comes from meeting someone who has experienced life in a similar way to yourself can be difficult to do accurately. The relationship may feel the same, especially as many spiritual lessons from previous lives don't surface immediately in a love relationship. Some spiritual lessons between partners don't surface until the closing moments of a relationship, as they deal with unresolved issues from the closing moments of a relationship between the partners in previous lifetimes.

In other cases I've seen couples settle together in order for a soul-mate child to be born, as the lesson for one or both partners involved the child. In this way destiny drew them together but not for a lesson directly between the partners. This is still a karmic love relationship but the partners are not necessarily soul mates.

If the shared history between partners is a negative history, it can still in some cases be positive, in that it helps them to bond initially. However, it can have a negative impact if they act out their history within their relationship. An example of this occurred with Shane and Marlene.

Shane grew up with a father who flew into a rage at least daily and his mother fought back until she grew too weary and eventually surrendered to his father's bullying. Marlene's parents were very similar and when she met Shane they felt at home with one another instantly. Soon the rows began and at first Marlene gave as good as she got, refusing to give in as her mother had done. This increased the intensity of the anger Shane felt and the rows escalated into scenes involving broken crockery, ornaments and windows. Eventually Marlene grew weary of the constant rows and she found herself surrendering to keep the peace and to preserve her sanity. The same pattern that initially made them feel at home with one another had started to destroy their trust and eventually their relationship. This is an extreme example, however, as many relationships are based around more subtle patterns.

Perhaps you share the same blind spots as your partner. An example of this might be if both partners agree that she'll ignore his philandering, and he'll agree to ignore her gambling addiction, and on it goes.

In an even more subtle form, perhaps both partners are prepared to accept the roles they are encouraged into at the start of a relationship. An example of this is Pieter, who is usually the emotional partner in a relationship. When he met Andrea he soon realised that she was far more overtly emotional than he, and he became the model of a practical, earthy man of few words. The more hysterical Andrea became, the more devoid of emotion Pieter became. Each realised the role they were to play and they fulfilled their roles as though they were a pair of dancers.

Chapter Nineteen

THE SOUL MATES QUESTIONNAIRE

I SENT THE FOLLOWING QUESTIONNAIRE OUT TO BOTH FRIENDS AND STRANGERS, AND THEN PASSED IT ON TO MORE PEOPLE AS A MEANS OF DISCOVERING WHAT PEOPLE THOUGHT AND FELT ABOUT THEIR SOUL-MATE LOVE RELATIONSHIPS.

As the responses flowed back to me from around the world, there were some surprising results. One respondent mentioned that she started the questionnaire as a laugh but soon found herself reviewing her past love relationships more seriously, asking herself if she had ever been in love with someone she considered a soul mate. Another woman wrote that when reviewing her soul-mate love relationship of some years ago, she realised that life had not been the same for her since then, and she promptly phoned her former partner to invite him for dinner. Things are progressing between them.

Sometimes by reflecting upon past actions and opportunities, we can clarify what will fulfil us in the future. The consistent theme in the responses to this questionnaire was that many people felt that they had squandered opportunities for love. I repeatedly read of how respondents regretted not making more of an opportunity to love and be loved by someone who was very special to them.

Perhaps in completing this questionnaire, you'll discover your own unresolved issues from past love relationships or illuminate regrets for past actions or inaction in the face of opportunities.

Questionnaire

This questionnaire is part of my research on soul mates, who, as I see it, are people whose life paths are shared for a period of time in order to learn spiritual lessons. I believe that soul mates can be friends, lovers, family members or business partners.

Confirmation of a soul-mates friendship or love relationship may be found in the intensity of that relationship from the start, or in the inner knowledge that destiny had a hand in bringing you together. Your definition of a soul mate may differ from this and if so, I'm happy for you to describe what a soul mate is to you in the space allowed at the end of the questionnaire.

The questions below refer to love relationships you have had, or are presently involved in. You'll need a pen and paper for this exercise.

1. Have you ever met someone you considered to be your soul mate?
2. How did you know that you were soul mates?
3. How did you meet?
4. Were there any obstacles to you being together?
5. Were relatives or friends opposed to your relationship?
6. How long have you been/were you together?
7. What do you consider has been the biggest lesson for you in this relationship?

8. What is your biggest regret with this relationship?

9. How did you know that this was an important love relationship?

10. Did you have to give up anything or anyone to be with this person?

11. Is there, or was there, any recurring issue within this relationship that you'd like to resolve?

12. In what ways does or did this relationship feed you emotionally, mentally and spiritually?

13. Have you spent any prolonged periods of time apart from one another during this relationship?

14. How was this for you?

15. How has this relationship helped to shape your life?

16. Do you regret not having pursued a different path in life due to this relationship?

17. What do/might you miss most about your soul mate if they were not in your life?

18. How do you deal with your partner's habits and beliefs that you don't like?

19. Did you receive any signs that your soul mate was approaching before you met? (For example, dreams etc.)

20. What do you feel is the primary lesson between you both?

21. How does that relationship compare with previous or subsequent relationships?

22. Was this person the type of person you had imagined yourself being in a relationship with when you were young?

23. How do you feel that others benefited from your relationship?

24. What do you see as your partner or friend's lesson in this relationship?

Putting your thoughts and realisations on paper can clarify your thinking process and underline your thoughts and feelings about a subject. Thinking something and seeing it written can be very different in the impact they have upon your mind.

The responses to this questionnaire surprised me. A common

theme soon emerged among those who had loved and lost a soul mate. They felt that it was important to seize opportunities for real love when they came along, moving mountains if necessary, in order to be with the right person.

Reading through the responses, it was evident that soul-mate love relationships don't run any more smoothly than usual love relationships, especially when one partner feels the urge to run away from the possibility of being loved on such a deep level. Why would someone choose to run away from something that feels so good and has the potential to be so rewarding? There are many reasons, primary among them being that they may feel that they have to surrender parts of themselves or their lives in order to be with a partner. Add to this such things as pride, ambition, terror at revealing yourself to another person in case they betray you, and unconscious attempts at sabotaging any opportunities for love, and you probably have more than half the adult population.

I was in awe, reading the hardships faced by people I didn't know, whose desire to be with the one they loved motivated them to endure deep, searing pain, abandonment and loss in the hope of being or remaining together.

One woman waited 16 years for circumstances to allow her to be with the man she knew to be her soul mate. Since that time he has left her more than a dozen times, and after she conceded that perhaps it was not to be this lifetime, they have reunited and are happy together. She felt that her lesson was to learn how to be alone without being lonely and she has struggled with this lesson since meeting that man when she was only 14 years of age. Now in her forties, she has found peace at last.

Reading through the questionnaires offered a glimpse into the lives of strangers, and in the brief pages I found examples of real emotional courage that are detailed in Chapter 22, 'More Examples from Life'. Naturally details have been changed to protect the privacy of those who generously responded.

Chapter Twenty

STAYING BEYOND
THE LESSON

WHEN YOU HAVE MASTERED THE LESSON THAT DREW YOU BOTH TOGETHER OR YOU HAVE PASSED THE POINT WHERE YOU CAN LEARN IT THIS LIFETIME WITH YOUR PARTNER, YOU HAVE NEW CHOICES. You can remain together in a love relationship without the karmic obligations or you can choose to move on to a single life or to another relationship.

Each situation is individual, so there is no right or wrong here. Many love relationships thrive without urgent underlying lessons, and it is possible to pursue your spiritual learning with friends, business partners or through your career. A relationship is only one option for learning spiritual lessons.

Sometimes partners feel the need to move on to another relationship soon after a lesson has been mastered, but this can also cause more pain than is necessary. Such was the case with Lauren and Tony. As soon as Lauren identified the underlying lesson in her relationship with Tony, she worked at mastering the lesson, which was trust. Lauren reunited this lifetime with Tony to remember that some men are reliable and trustworthy. Another part of her, however, longed to spend time with a more exciting man, despite realising that sometimes more exciting men were less reliable in love relationships. Soon after accepting that Tony was responsible and reliable, Lauren left him for a relationship with Aldo, whom she found more unpredictable and passionate. Although it appeared that her lesson with Tony was complete, Tony was very shaken by her sudden decision to leave and it took him more than five years to open up to love again.

Although there was nothing obvious to be gained by Lauren staying with Tony, Lauren may have caused more pain than was strictly necessary by leaving suddenly. Realistically it is impossible to know fully what motivated Lauren to leave Tony as suddenly as she did, but she described it as 'having the feeling that we were becoming friends instead of lovers'.

'Was that such a bad thing?' I asked her, and she nodded pensively. Tony and Lauren are still friends but sometimes when a karmic or soul-mates love relationship concludes after the lessons are learned, the partners have little or no contact with each other, as nothing draws them together again. Only circumstances and those involved can determine whether it is wise to remain in a soul-mates relationship after you feel you've mastered your spiritual lessons together.

At the risk of justifying brief love affairs, it is possible to meet and to learn a lesson rapidly, then part company, just as it is possible to meet and recognise a soul mate, before determining that there is nothing to learn from one another together this lifetime. Recognising that your actions have consequences is often enough to make you careful in how you treat others, especially those who love you, even if you don't return their feelings.

A parent who thwarts their child's ambition to pursue a particular life direction can be setting themself up for a great deal of suffering later on as a result of their actions. Aside from the karmic implications of creating a lesson to be mastered together at some later point, they risk sabotaging their relationship with their child in later years. The parent-child relationship is probably the most powerful of all relationships, and it has the potential to be the most influential in a single lifetime.

When my son was born, I recognised his spirit and I knew within that he'd been my parent, my friend and my business partner in previous lives, and that this time around I was charged with the shared responsibility of helping him to reach adulthood safely and with a broad understanding of life. His mother is also keen to help widen his view of life, to the point where she has travelled to Europe with him four times on extended holidays, and all before the age of seven.

I recognise that our relationship is that of parent and child this lifetime, and yet his subconscious recall of our times together as adults makes him resist taking direction from me, as he is used to us being equals. In another 15 years we will be equal as adults again and our karma together will continue in new ways.

Although the karma between his mother and I has concluded and we have separated, our karma with him is not yet complete and he'll hopefully be content to learn his lesson with us this lifetime.

Realising that this is only a small part of a greater picture helps to increase perspective which is useful when you are experiencing searing pain caused by yourself or your partner. This doesn't necessarily diminish the pain, but it can help you to realise that this won't last forever. This, too, will pass.

If we are all in the business of building boats, then our relationships take on a new perspective. We build a boat together or we work on improving each other's existing boats, as we teach one another and hopefully learn from one another.

The essential lessons are contained in the karmic attraction to one another (or repulsion in some cases, depending on our history together), but after the lessons are complete, we are free to remain with one another for life or for any period of time we choose. The only noticeable difference is that you may not feel the same urgency to be together that you felt before you mastered your lessons within the relationship.

In some cases, although you are in a relationship together, one partner refuses to learn or to grow, and this prevents the other partner from mastering their lesson and moving on to a more rewarding love relationship. There is no rule stating that both partners have to be ready, willing and able to pursue their opportunities for spiritual growth and development.

An example of this occurred recently with Meredith, whose marriage to Dirk had concluded after only four months. Meredith was devastated when Dirk told her that he had never loved her and that he was leaving her. He made it clear to Meredith that he was seeking a divorce and she was reeling when she consulted me. I scanned their situation to see the spiritual lessons between them, and I noticed another simple lesson that had no karmic significance, but which Meredith had to master before she would have a long-lasting stable love relationship.

Meredith had a fondness for younger men who were often passionate and undisciplined. In her late thirties, Meredith found men in their early twenties very attractive, despite their emotional immaturity. When I questioned her about this, she became defensive and I had to reassure her that I was not moralising but instead pointing out that 'boys will be boys'. Although they may find marriage appealing, it is unlikely that they will have thought through the implications of a long-term relationship carefully.

At this point Meredith's eyes filled with tears.

'Look, I understand that you like cute young men, and it's obvious that they like you, too, judging by your last three relationships,' I said to her in a compassionate tone. 'But perhaps you can have relationships with them without expecting them to be grown up and responsible. Let's face it. If they were grown up and responsible, you'd probably find them a bit dull.' She laughed at this and nodded as I continued. 'I have heard that desk-bound men in their thirties don't usually have the same rock hard buttocks as 23-year-olds who spend their days swimming and working out a the gym.'

'You bet they don't,' she laughed.

'On the other hand, men in their early twenties don't usually have the maturity and ability to commit themselves to long-term relationships as men in their thirties. I'm generalising here, but you get the point don't you?'

'Yes, I do,' she said.

'Now to your karmic lessons with Dirk. He's not likely to come back so perhaps you can learn them with him as a friend this lifetime. It has the feeling of right people but wrong timing this lifetime I'm afraid.'

'So what were the lessons?' she asked. I paused and clairvoyantly scanned for the answer.

'It's a bit complicated,' I said at last. 'You have tried twice so far to build a business together to enable you both to be free from financial restrictions, but each time you have not fulfilled your plans to your satisfaction. In this lifetime it seems that he wasn't ready for the commitment such a challenge requires.'

'Well you have one thing right. He was always hopeless with money.'

'And how are you with financial plans and commitments?'

'Er, not that good actually. I'll be paying off the wedding for at least two years yet.'

How do you tell your soul mate that you love them?

Often it's not enough to know that we care for our soul mates, they have to be reminded of how we regard them. Whether they are lovers, friends or family members, they need to be reminded regularly for several reasons. Firstly, friends and relationship partners usually respond well when it is confirmed to them that they are loved and appreciated. Secondly, you cannot be sure when you will see your soul mate for the last time in this life, so to avoid living with regret that you left things unsaid to your soul mate, it pays to tell them how you feel.

While that's the theory, in reality we can hold back from expressing our innermost feelings for a variety of reasons. Sometimes we are afraid that we won't always feel as we do when we express our feelings to another. We may also be afraid of appearing foolish if our feelings are not returned. I read recently of an example of the reverse of this where a couple in their seventies ensured that they always kissed one another goodbye properly whenever they parted, even for the day. Several times the husband phoned his wife on her mobile phone to ask her to return home to kiss him goodbye when she had left in a hurry. It was just as well, for he suffered a heart attack and died when she was out visiting friends one day.

Too often we await the perfect moment to tell our soul mate how we feel, but it rarely, if ever, comes. Words are only one way of showing someone how valuable they are to you and even those words don't have to be the obvious ones. An example of this is my seven-year-old son, who loves being told stories. He is content to hear a favourite story many times, partly because he enjoys the time we spend together laughing, and partly because it holds echoes of the first time he heard it and laughed heartily. When I tell him a story about a caterpillar that refused to climb trees because it didn't like heights, he knows that he is important to me because I am spending time with him doing what he likes to do – to laugh.

While some people respond well to words and to stories, others prefer actions. One couple demonstrate their love for each other through food. Nigel loves to cook and Liz spends hours at a time searching for the perfect wine to present to Nigel. While Nigel is at home roasting some game and tending to a hearty soup, Liz is deep in discussion with the owner of a local liquor store, arguing the merits of different wines to accompany dinner. They claim to have sampled 74 different brands and types of chocolate between them, often washed down with cognac.

Some people confirm their love for their soul mates with surprises, but these can lead to disappointment, as was often the case with John and Naomi. John loved to surprise Naomi with outrageous gifts that required Naomi to be spontaneous, which by nature she wasn't. When she refused to use his gift voucher to ride in a Tiger Moth aeroplane because it didn't have a roof, he was shattered. I tried to point out that he had not asked himself what Naomi might like but instead had given her something that he would have liked to do. John reasoned that asking Naomi what she wanted defeated the purpose of a surprise until it was suggested that perhaps Naomi didn't even like surprises. In time John was able to demonstrate his love for her after asking Naomi what she wanted.

Surprises work for some people, as in the case of Theo and Carlos. Carlos worked from home and Theo was able to slip away from work occasionally to surprise Carlos. His surprises varied from a spontaneous picnic to tickets on an interstate flight for the weekend and Carlos loved these surprises.

Sometimes all your soul mate needs to be reassured that they are loved and appreciated is to be touched. From a brief hug to gentle strokes, some partners respond immediately to being touched. An example of this is Nicci, who is regularly called upon to massage her partner's neck and shoulders. Her partner, Brenton, explained that Nicci's touch is soothing and that he can sense her love for him and her dedication to the task at hand when she massages him.

When touch doesn't work, you may need to be inventive or adaptable. Christopher found that Kirstin didn't respond to his touch, to his words or to flowers, despite being in a love relationship for two years. Then he accidentally discovered the way to her heart when she was laid up in bed with a bad cold. As a surprise for lunch one day, he sent a food parcel around to her, containing a three-course hot meal, some pate, soft cheese, cracker biscuits, a large bunch of dark grapes, a punnet of strawberries, two sweet pastries and a bottle of red wine. Kirstin was overjoyed by the gesture and scoffed most of the contents of the parcel before Christopher arrived home from work that evening. Despite her ill health, Kirstin was in high spirits when Christopher saw her (and no, she had not opened the red wine). These days, instead of sending flowers or perfume, Christopher insists upon sending only edible presents to Kirstin, to remind her that he loves her. He suggests that the food reaches those parts of Kirstin that hugging and romantic words don't reach!

Looking closely at your soul mates to determine what they

might appreciate is essential if you don't want to give them a gift that they are too polite to refuse. I have a friend, Angela, who has a house bursting with gifts from well-meaning friends, which conflict with her own taste. Angela is too polite to give unwanted gifts away and to train her into the habit, I decided to give her a gift that she didn't like, couldn't use and which was sure to clash with everything else in her house. I searched for three weeks until I came across the perfect gift. It was a bright purple plastic wine cooler, and considering that Angela doesn't drink wine, it was a good start. As she unwrapped it I told her that she was free to give it away to anyone she felt deserving of it and within 30 minutes the next-door neighbour stopped in to return a bowl he had borrowed earlier. Angela seized the moment and offered the wine cooler to him and he accepted. We laughed heartily afterwards. It occurred to me later that to give Angela a gift that I was sure she liked, I'd have to wait for her to purchase something herself and then offer to refund her costs. As she was a gracious recipient of presents, it was the only way to ensure she was happy with a gift.

Sometimes the perfect way to tell a soul mate that you love and appreciate them is to give them some time away from you or from those around them. From a weekend away to rest and relax, to a trip back to their home town or their homeland, the gift of time to be alone can be precious indeed to some people.

Alternately, the gift of time together can also prove a valuable way of telling a soul mate that you love them. It need not be an expensive holiday overseas or even a long period of time. It might be as simple as dinner for two and a stroll along your favourite beach on a late summer's evening, or a weekend away from work commitments to spend time together doing those simple things that make up most of our lives. In the 1980s and 90s, the term 'quality time' gained currency but in reality it is all quality time. If you miss spending time together today, you will never experience this day again. If you wait for the perfect time to tell someone close to you that you love them, you will probably miss a thousand perfect times, perceiving tiny imperfections in the myriad moments that float past you every week. I have seen too many retired clients who don't really know their children and grandchildren because they had been too busy just living to notice those around them who made a difference to their lives.

As it is rare to know when someone that you love is about to die, it is better to say whatever you need to now, before you have to live with regret. Sometimes we are afraid to say what we feel to those we love the most, for fear of embarrassment or not always feeling as we do at present. Perhaps this accounts for the popularity of love songs, for they may express what we feel we cannot say aloud.

By observing your soul mates, you can discover what language speaks to them. They may be easily reached through touch, through words, flowers, food, laughter or through bungy jumping from a bridge late at night. If you tell them that you care in a language that reaches them, you have an opportunity to deepen your relationship with them. Most of us seek recognition from those we care about that we are valued by them, and yet few of us know how we like to be reminded. How do you like to be reminded that you are valued by your friends, family and your soul mates?

Exercise

1. How do you demonstrate your love for your soul mates?
2. What is your soul mate's name?
3. List the ways in which you show them that you care for them.
4. How do you like to have confirmation that you are loved and appreciated?
5. In the past, how have you enjoyed being told that you are loved?
6. How do you dream of being told that you are loved and appreciated?
7. Do those close to you now know how you like to be told that you are loved?
8. If not, how can you tell them?

Chapter Twenty One

WHY DO WE SEEK SOUL-MATE RELATIONSHIPS?

❦

O N THE SURFACE, MANY PEOPLE ARE LONELY AND THEY SEEK SOMEONE WHO'LL UNDERSTAND THEM ON A DEEPER LEVEL THAN THEY HAVE EXPERIENCED, AND IN THESE CASES THE SEARCH FOR A SOUL MATE IS OFTEN THE SEARCH FOR UNDERSTANDING. For many people a soul-mate relationship represents a chance for unconditional love. It offers a chance to be loved; warts and all.

On a deeper level, our spirits seek to evolve in order to return from whence they came. On some level, a part of you remembers that you are more than your physical body and that there are lessons to be mastered. That deeper part recognises that you have chosen a physical body in order to increase your restrictions and make the lesson more difficult, and in turn, a more valued prize.

Imagine for a moment that you were given a challenge, but in order to make that challenge more difficult, you were also given some basic restrictions. You were given a physical body that required food, water, sleep and that it be kept within a certain temperature range for continued survival. To further complicate the challenge, you agree to consciously forget the task set for you as you come to grips with mastering the mechanics of the physical body.

By the time you have slept a thousand nights, you have learned to walk, to talk and to communicate on a basic level with your species. Much of your waking time is spent feeding and maintaining your physical, emotional and mental bodies. Just when you feel that life is perfect, along comes a younger brother or sister, and the adults at home suddenly have less time to devote to you. At this point your emotional needs are foremost, but you soon realise that you can meet many of these needs with people the same size as yourself, at day care or kindergarten.

Without your parents or other adults to remind you that you are more than your physical body, and to give you a hint of where you fit in the universal scheme of things, you may reach adulthood having ignored the challenge set for you before you entered your physical body.

Then as an adolescent or a young adult, you fall in love. You have great hopes and plans that this love will fill that dull ache that seems to be growing steadily within you. Love or the yearning for love has awoken you to a part of your purpose, and reminded you of a time when there was no yearning. Unconsciously, your challenge has presented itself and you then meet people who can teach you things that you will need in order to complete your challenge successfully.

This is similar to the tale of the Sleeping Beauty. In the tale she falls asleep for a hundred years (asleep to her spiritual purpose for many lifetimes) until her prince (her soul mate) arrives to remind her of her true purpose. She no doubt reminds him of his own purpose in turn, for his quest is to find the person who remembers his spiritual purpose.

Another version of Adam and Eve suggests that Eve reminded Adam of his true purpose, and that Adam has not yet forgiven her for it, as evidenced by the more popular version of the story where she tempts him from his purpose.

It can be a lonely path taking a life in a human body, and there are many expensive diversions from the innate loneliness such as entertainment, travel, films, books, computer games, drugs and alcohol, but when these diversions have subsided, you may still feel alone. The search for a deep, loving relationship with someone who can dispel that innate loneliness is often a long and sometimes painful one. Partners may dispel that dull ache for a week, a month or even 25 years, but unless you recognise your spiritual purpose and follow that purpose, you will feel alone again eventually.

Taking your spiritual purpose into account, it is fair to say that soul mates are often there to remind us of our purpose. They are fellow travellers on the path and all of us need reminders from time to time. Years ago after the conclusion of a love relationship, I sank into a deep depression. As is often the case, I lost motivation for social things. I ignored my friends and sat around staring at the walls. A good friend who worked nearby appeared at the front door one afternoon and invited me snorkelling. We drove to the beach and he provided me with a snorkel. The water was cold but refreshing, and within a few minutes I had forgotten my own problems, as I discovered a whole, new world beneath the surface of the sea. Three of four times a week that summer, Chris knocked at my front door and together we snorkelled in the late afternoon sun. It was a healing experience second to none, and it occurred to me later that Chris recognised that although he was powerless to heal me of my recent loss, he was able to help me to rebalance myself, through snorkelling. Chris reminded me that there are other experiences awaiting me and another world which had been invisible to me, such as the underwater world of snorkelling, opened up.

At first I bent his ear with stories of my recent relationship and he patiently listened. After a month or so I found that I spoke less of my past partner and more of my life as it was. This is a classic example of a soul mate, in that they remind us of our deeper purpose, often without knowing it.

Chris was aware of what he was doing to help me and I am grateful to him for such practical assistance when I was desperately in need. However, soul mates often say or do things that help us to remember our purpose without ever being aware of the effects of their words or actions.

Sometimes even tactless words or reckless actions serve to awaken us to a lesson, although I hesitate to suggest that all such words or actions are reminders. Sometimes people are needlessly cruel and I guess that comes down to free will.

Our search for a soul-mate love relationship can be the result of a deeper need to be reminded of our spiritual purpose this lifetime, or the need to resolve those issues and remove those obstacles that stand in the way of us realising our goals this lifetime. Although others are sometimes an excellent reminder or a motivation for spiritual growth and development, this is not the only way to be reminded.

If a deeper part of each of us knows our true purpose, then it makes sense to contact that deeper part, in order to remind ourselves where we are heading this lifetime. Although it is tempting to seek the counsel or guidance of others in the search for purpose, I argue that all others can really do is to remind us of what we already know on some deeper level.

This is not to discount the value of being reminded by others of our true spiritual purpose, but using others to remind us can be expensive and time-consuming. What may take an outsider 10 years to teach you might be learned in a year or two through a simpler method.

Now that I have your attention, you'll be asking yourself what technique could shave years off your learning time and allow you to advance yourself spiritually. So allow me to describe the technique before I give you its more common name.

If that still, small voice within is being drowned out by the more vocal demands of your mind, your heart and your physical body, you need to quiet those other voices, even temporarily, in order to hear that inner voice. It is impossible to permanently still your mind, your heart and your physical needs, but there are many techniques by which you can temporarily still those voices.

I was able to still those voices temporarily through snorkelling in the sea, but this technique is less likely to be pursued in a cold, bleak winter. You can sometimes still these other voices during sleep, but the results of listening to your inner voice are sometimes forgotten upon awakening as you rush on into your day.

For many of us, one voice is often louder and more persistent than the others. If you have a health problem, perhaps your physical body is calling more loudly than the other voices. If you have suffered a great emotional loss, it is likely that your emotional voice is dominating your awareness as you struggle to quiet your emotions. If you are attempting to make sense of life or to understand why events have occurred in your life, perhaps your mental voice is more dominant.

Each of these voices needs to be quietened in order to hear that deep spiritual voice within which knows from whence you came and where you are going. This voice may present as an instinct, a dream, a deep longing or repetitive thoughts. If your needs are pressing, it may be impossible to quiet those physical, emotional and mental desires in order to hear that deeper, spiritual voice, and this was the case with Valerie.

Valerie was suffering great physical pain on a daily basis as she struggled with stomach cancer. It was pointless my asking her to go within for the life direction she sought, as her pain was screaming at her, despite the high dosages of prescribed pain-killers. In those brief periods of respite from the pain, Valerie fell asleep from sheer exhaustion.

I offered to go within for her, to find what might help her to quiet her physical voice, or reduce the physical pain. What I was told by my inner voice was that Valerie required brief periods of concentration upon other things, and that during these periods she'd be open to her spiritual voice. I asked what sort of brief periods of concentration and I was told to simply take her into the garden and to spend a minute examining some jasmine on the fence that had just begun to flower. It seemed such a small and insignificant thing to do in the face of her illness and her looming possible death, but I proceeded to do as I was shown. Half an hour later, we stood outside watching a spray of flowers when a bee arrived and we observed it collecting honey from the flowers and pollinating them at the same time.

'Life just goes on,' Valerie said in a puzzled voice. 'I'm looking at possible death and life still goes on all around me. Look at this bee. It goes on about its business as though it were another sunny day. It is another sunny day in fact, and I'm standing here facing possible death.'

Silence fell again and we stood tracing the bee's movements with our gaze as the sun beat down on our backs. It was warm and the still air made it cosy, but her words echoed around in my head, chilling me in the early spring sunshine. A breeze stirred and the scent of jasmine engulfed us.

'...facing possible death,' I thought, and I struggled for something to say. There are no words for someone facing possible death except one of the words she had said aloud to me.

'Possible,' I said aloud and she took my arm and burst into tears.

'You're right,' she sobbed. 'It is only possible after all. I mean look at these bees. They know their place in the greater scheme of things. They collect honey and they pollinate and they feed the bees back at the hive. That's it! They know their place. Where is my place? What am I doing here? I'm standing in the garden waiting for the morphine to kick in and numb the constant pain.'

She composed herself and sighed. Several more bees hovered into view and began working their way through the flowering jasmine. I cleared my throat and spoke slowly.

'I don't know your place in the greater scheme of things, but right now... right now you are standing in the garden with me, and we're watching the workings of nature. Right now we can see more about the purpose of these bees than they can probably see for themselves.'

'So why do you think I can see the purpose of a bloody bee and yet my own life is still a mystery to me?'

Her arm rested on my forearm and she steadied herself on the uneven ground. I was giving her all the support I could at that stage, by steadying her on her feet in the garden.

'I guess the difference between your awareness of the bees and yourself is perspective. You have an objective perspective regarding the bees and you see more as a result.'

'Oh that's just great. So I have to leave my body to obtain an objective perspective.'

'Not necessarily. For a moment here we were staring at the bees and these flowers, and I lost all awareness of myself, and my physical and emotional needs. Did that occur with you too?'

She pondered this for a moment.

'Yes. Yes it did come to think of it,' she replied. I felt a sense of peace sweep over me. Perhaps I had been of some small help after all? Then she continued.

'So what you're saying is that to achieve brief moments of respite from the physical pain and the emotional and mental anguish, I have to stand out here in the garden staring a these damned bees and flowers?'

I looked at her for a moment and then I laughed. 'And on the seventh day, God created bickering,' I said. Valerie grinned at this and I seized the moment. 'That makes two times since we've been standing our here that you've forgotten your fears and your anguish. Only briefly, I admit, but you forgot them nonetheless.'

I could only imagine how hard it was for Valerie to quiet her mind and her emotions in order to hear the deeper voice within, but most of us don't have such pressing concerns, and yet we fail to hear the inner voice.

The technique which is a most powerful method for listening to your inner voice is meditation. Meditation offers an opportunity to quiet the mind and to hear your spiritual voice while still conscious. Meditation requires practice, but usually a lot less practice than learning to walk or to speak.

I often hear from people about how they've tried to meditate but that they couldn't do it. I point out that the state of meditation is between wakefulness and sleep, so they pass in and out of this state at least twice a day. It is not an unusual or strange state to enter, and the body is familiar with it.

Meditation often improves with the right motivation. If you had the choice of spending five hours a week for three months learning to meditate (a total of 65 hours over 13 weeks), or spending five hours a day struggling with a relationship that is causing you great stress or loneliness (a total of 455 hours over 13 weeks), which would you choose?

The first option increases your chances of understanding what you can learn from your circumstances whereas the second only offers you pain and frustration with the possibility of reasoning a way out. It's a safe bet that most people would opt for the option that increases the chances of reducing the stress or pain.

The part of you that remembers your purpose cannot speak up so you need to make things quiet enough for it to be easily heard. Meditation offers you that stillness and quiet. Not every time you meditate, but eventually often enough to spare you circumstances which might cause you great pain. There are many types of meditation, from focusing on a lighted candle flame and chanting a mantra to moving meditations, and through experimenting you can find a few which suit you.

Several step-by-step meditations have been outlined in *A Secret Door to the Universe* for readers who are unfamiliar with meditation. For the more meditation-resistant, I am currently making up a meditation CD that offers several guided meditations for improved intuition and spiritual development. (See website in Index.) Even those with restless minds can benefit from guided meditations, until they feel confident to meditate independently.

A meditation course may benefit you as it is easier to slip into a natural state of meditation when you are surrounded by a group of people who are meditating. When people meditate in groups, it is easier to be swept up into meditation with the group energy and it offers beginners higher meditations than might otherwise be experienced alone.

Chapter Twenty Two

MORE EXAMPLES FROM LIFE

Learning about love from a soul mate

WHEN PEOPLE SEEK A SOUL MATE THEY ARE USUALLY SEEKING TO BE LOVED, BUT ONE RESPONDENT DESCRIBED THE BIGGEST LESSON IN HER SOUL MATE FRIENDSHIP WAS ALLOWING SOMEONE TO LOVE HER. Adrianna found that loving her friend Casey was easy but when Casey attempted to show Adrianna how she was valued, Adrianna felt very uncomfortable. Many years after Casey's death, Adrianna passionately described how Casey taught her to accept friendship, love and simple affection. In giving up her social life to nurse Casey, Adrianna felt that she was in turn gaining a better quality of life for herself.

In the closing months of her life, the disdain Casey was shown by those responsible for her welfare tore Adrianna apart emotionally, and in the final months when Casey was unable to speak, she appeared often in Adrianna's night-time dreams to communicate her needs and her appreciation for their friendship.

Upon reflection, Adrianna felt that her friendship with Casey taught her how to love and to be loved in return. As a result it has deepened her friendships with others and with her husband.

Casey had appeared to Adrianna in a dream the day before they met, and in the dream, Casey was accompanied by Adrianna's deceased mother, who held Casey's hand as though they were old friends. After Casey's death, Adrianna recalled the dream and remarked that it was as though her mother was introducing them. The dream made Casey's death easier to bear, as Adrianna feels that Casey has joined her mother in spirit, and this has been confirmed to her through repeated dreams of the two of them, happily together.

Learning from past experience in love

Respondents described age differences of eight to 18 years, confirming that real love knows few boundaries. Surprisingly, several respondents resisted having a love relationship with an older man (even six years older) despite strong feelings of attraction to the person.

Many people detailed frustrating first marriages that left them wary of new relationships. It occurred to me that these long relationships with controlling and jealous partners may have resulted in people being more appreciative of their soul mates for the smoothness of their time together.

Children from previous marriages often caused havoc, which is understandable, as a new partner means a new person with whom they must share their parent. Sometimes the children involved saw their parent for a limited time each month so they were understandably demanding during their visits.

Those responding to the questionnaire repeatedly wrote of mutual support of each other's interests and pursuits, such as study, career choices and even places to live in the world. This didn't prevent either partner from being themselves, nor did it appear to stifle their independence. Some wrote of initial struggles to be themselves before negotiations took place that allowed their relationships to become more workable and rewarding for both partners.

Sharing the path together

Although soul-mate love relationships aren't without upheaval, resolutions seemed to come for almost all of those who responded to the questionnaire, whereas previous love relationships for many of them were as competitive and fraught with struggle at the start as at the end. It was as though after struggling with relationships that were going nowhere, these people have found someone who actually shares the path they currently tread. It is reassuring to see partners with a different history, and possibly a different ending point, happily sharing a path together.

An intuitive link

Most people wrote of an intuitive link between one another and one respondent, Stephen, was uneasy about his partner, Benita, being able to 'read' his emotions from far away. He described how he felt unable to hide from her intuitive gaze, and when he was feeling angry or frustrated, Benita intuitively knew to leave him alone. When emotional issues unrelated to their relationship surfaced within Stephen, he felt the need to shield Benita from the resultant emotional turbulence and although they lived and worked on different sides of the city, she was always able to know where he was emotionally.

'Boys like a few secrets,' he argued, while she stated that 'Girls like communication, so talk to me.' Over the years Stephen learned that as Benita was aware of his innermost feelings anyway, he might as well tell her what he was thinking and feeling. Soon he discovered that she was often able to help him put his feelings into perspective, and their relationship deepened as a result.

Fear of rejection

I read of people whose fear of being hurt prevented them from surrendering to their feelings at the start, and these people listed this as their single greatest regret regarding their soul-mate love relationships. It is understandable when previous painful relationships are taken into account, and the fact that several people wrote of feeling previously strongly attracted to someone who did not return their feelings.

In one case, Linda was so afraid of expressing the depth of her feeling for Reg that she held back until they separated. Now, six years later, Reg is married to someone else and Linda has not found anyone who matches him in her mind. She described living daily with the regret of not finding the courage to pursue a relationship that she felt to be right for her. In completing the questionnaire, Linda discovered feelings for Reg that she had buried, which left her reassessing her emotional life direction.

Dreams about a forthcoming soulmate

Before actually meeting Reg, Linda had dreamed of meeting him and the two of them ending up together. When they met, they developed a friendship for a year and a half before launching into a deep love relationship. Those dreams haunted her as she felt too young to be settling down. She was afraid that she might miss out on a better offer for a love relationship later on if she settled down with Reg in her twenties.

Now in her early thirties, Linda perceives that she was simply given a good opportunity too soon to recognise it for what it was. Having experienced three relationships since separating from Reg, Linda described them as nowhere near the intensity of her relationship with Reg.

How many of us seek to be loved in theory but run from the arms of love in reality? Linda described it as never feeling as loved or as secure in her relationships after separating from Reg. Subsequent men carried with them an echo of Reg for Linda, and unable to shake the memory of him, Linda spent a few years alone to determine exactly what she wanted in a partner.

Family opposition

People also detailed family opposition to their soul-mate love relationships and I guess you can usually count on someone in your family to disagree with your choices and to verbalise their disagreement. This can be a healthy thing, as sometimes family members point out practical reasons why a relationship won't work. Different cultural backgrounds can test the most ardent love, and sometimes ruin a relationship, but with adaptability and persistence, you may stand a good chance of going beyond your life experience to forge a relationship without a traditional mould.

With this in mind, family members who tell you that it is not wise to pursue such a love relationship probably mean well. They may not want to see you hurt when family or cultural pressure results in difficult circumstances.

Expectations

Another recurring point about soul-mate love relationships is that many respondents felt that their relationships survived so well because they did not expect one another to share their tastes, hobbies and interests. While romantic novels set the scene of love lasting forever because a couple have everything in common, reality paints a different picture.

When partners have varying interests, these can lead to a tug of war over time spent together, or it can lead to each partner refreshing themselves with new experiences that they can bring back to their relationship. Allowing your soul-mate partner to have different perceptions of life can be the beginning of a beautiful relationship.

An example of allowing for the natural differences between partners occurred with Max, whose partner liked horse riding. As my partner also loved to ride, the girls spent many Saturday afternoons out riding while Max and I stayed at home preparing dinner. In fact Max cooked dinner and I made margaritas. Before long we were joined by Sean, whose partner also rode horses, and the three of us had some great conversations, sumptuous lunches and marvellous margaritas. By the evening meal, all of us had done what we wanted with our day, and we were all refreshed. The following day, however, we all ached; the girls from riding and the boys from drinking. Sundays were generally quiet days.

Seeking a partner who shares all of your interests can become stifling after awhile. Partners in healthy soul-mate relationships often benefit from time spent apart doing things with other people.

Relationship loyalty

Having a loyal partner and trusting that person is essential if you plan to spend time apart, so that you can comfortably focus on the interests you have, without fearing the worst about your partner while they are out of your sight. To help you to keep your relationship in perspective, it may be necessary to recall that you are both building a boat, which you will use to sail away together or separately.

I have a friend who complains when I mention this fact, stating that she only wants a permanent relationship but I ask in return, 'What in life is permanent?' None of us will be here in our current form in 50 or 100 years, so permanent is merely a concept.

To help her to understand the limitations of her desires, I asked her to recall her first love relationship. She sighed as she remembered, and I asked her how it concluded.

'He cheated on me with my best friend,' she said bitterly.

'And how do you think life would be for you if he were still with you in a love relationship now?'

'I couldn't be with someone who wasn't faithful.'

'Have you always been faithful to your partners?'

'That's not fair. I only slept with other people when my relationships were well and truly over.'

'Over, meaning that you weren't relationship partners?' I asked.

'Pretty much, yes.'

'And did any of these 'no longer my real partner' partners feel betrayed when they found out that you had slept with another man?'

'Well, yes. But I never slept with their best friends like my first partner did.'

'No. You conveniently selected someone unknown to them to reduce any feelings of betrayal or loss they might experience at discovering that their soon-to-be-ex-partner was sleeping with another man before going home to them.'

'You make it sound so tawdry.'

'It is betrayal. It is no different to your first partner, and yet you made a list of qualities you sought in a man stating that you wanted him to be honest, trustworthy and faithful. By your own admission you are or have been none of these things, so how do you expect to find someone who has qualities you don't have within yourself?'

'So you're suggesting that I can only have a partner who has the same qualities as myself?' she asked me.

'Well look at it this way. How long do you think a love relationship might last if one partner is faithful, loyal and trustworthy while the other is unfaithful? My guess is that it will last as long as the faithful partner remains blind to the lack of commitment from their spouse.'

'Yes,' she sighed, 'but where does that leave someone wanting a soul-mate partner?'

'Perhaps it leaves them looking at themselves, to see what they are offering and what qualities they can bring to a love relationship.'

Chapter Twenty Three

A GLIMPSE OF THE SOUL'S PURPOSE

TO MORE READILY UNDERSTAND HOW WE LOSE OUR WAY ON OUR SPIRITUAL PATHS, WE NEED TO EXAMINE HOW THE MIND, THE SOUL AND THE BODY ARE INTERRELATED. The soul is bonded to the mind in this lifetime, whereas the mind is bonded to the body and each in turn drags the other down into life.

So the mind draws the spirit down into life through the mind's curiosity about life, and keeps it there through limiting beliefs about the nature of reality. The body draws the mind down deeper into life through demands of the senses and what started out as a question of, 'Where am I going in this lifetime?' soon becomes another question of 'What can I get from this person or situation?' Slowly, spiritual purpose is layered deep beneath material and emotional desires and the responsibilities for those things desired.

Eventually your vision of life is shortened by the demands of those things directly beneath your feet. Your workplace, your home, your car and the clothes you stand in. Although the physical body benefits from your acquiring and maintaining these things, your spirit may perish if untended too long.

If you accept the reasoning that we are here to master spiritual lessons, then soul mates are here to help us in the classroom. They offer us an opportunity to remember our soul's purpose, and to accept some help with our purpose or to help someone else with theirs. In remaining aware of the purpose of the soul, it can be easier to release the grip we have on some of our soul mates, knowing that what they have helped us to learn will live on within us long after they have gone from our lives. Our soul remembers them, so that if and when we cross paths again, a deep sense of recognition occurs within each of us, and if we are aware, we know that destiny is at hand, guiding us toward a lesson in the grand scheme of things.

To achieve this awareness, we need to resist the call of the body to the mind and the call of the mind to the soul, coaxing us to forget our true spiritual purpose and struggle the days away with material things. We need to encourage a sense of detachment from our daily responsibilities even for a few minutes each day, in order to see life's bigger picture. It is essential to keep in mind that days soon become weeks, and weeks become years before another life is spent in ignorance of the true purpose of the soul.

Although others accompany us on our spiritual path from time to time, only we can take all the necessary steps towards our own spiritual destination. As we say farewell to each soul mate who shared the path with us, we can look forward to seeing them again later down the path. Who knows, we may meet many of those we shared parts of the path with at the close of the journey.

If lifetimes are to enable us to learn spiritual lessons, then that final gathering at the end of all the different paths will be the ultimate school reunion. When you arrive you'll find me standing by the punch bowl.